# Folk Dancing

## FOR STUDENTS AND TEACHERS

# Folk Dancing

## FOR STUDENTS AND TEACHERS

**Second Edition**

CONSTANCE V. MYNATT
BERNARD D. KAIMAN

East Tennessee State University

WM. C. BROWN COMPANY PUBLISHERS
Dubuque, Iowa

PHYSICAL EDUCATION

Consulting Editor
Aileene Lockhart
Texas Woman's University

PARKS AND RECREATION

Consulting Editor
David Gray
California State University, Long Beach

HEALTH

Consulting Editor
Robert Kaplan
The Ohio State University

# Contents

## Couple And Mixer Dances



## Dances for Three or More



## 7. Dance Patterns—Moderately Easy to Learn . . . . . . . . . . . 73

### Non-Partner Dances



### Couple and Mixer Dances



### Dances For Three or More

Swedish

# *Preface*

We have made many changes in the second edition of this book, some of which will be described below; but we have not changed our goals. This book is written for the teacher of folk dance, the teacher-in-training, and the folk dance student. It is our aim to present the material so that each will be able to learn the dances more easily, to improve dance skills, to enjoy the dances, and to develop a sincere interest in folk dance, thus resulting in better teachers and students.

The instructor will find that the dances in this book are enjoyable to teach and are based on a variety of fundamental dance skills; together these present a reasonably comprehensive introduction to folk dancing as it is done both in the academic world and in the recreational field today. Nearly a third of the dances described in this book are found in the latest (1973) Folk Dance Popularity List of the California Folk Dance Federation (*Let's Dance,* Vol. 31, 2, 26-27; Feb., 1974). The dances are carefully described so that even unfamiliar dances can be readily worked out. Teaching methods as well as suggestions for the learner are discussed. Practical suggestions are given to help the teacher in his appraisal of folk dance proficiency, since in the school situation the ability of the students must be evaluated. The student will find specific suggestions for learning a dance and some general hints, which together with the dance instructions will make the learning process more efficient.

Both authors have been actively engaged in the teaching of folk dance for many years, and have come to realize the needs of the teacher-in-training and the limitations which beginning students bring with them to class. This experience, plus a wide acquaintance with many of the foremost folk dance teachers in the United States and the opportunity to study folk dancing while traveling in many foreign countries, has provided the background of this book.

In this edition, sixteen dances have been added, bringing the total of folk dances described to seventy-nine. The selection of the new material was based on our observations of the popularity which these dances presently enjoy in folk dance groups all over the United States and the interest of the students in our own campus classes as we introduced these "newer" folk dances. The sixteen dances also add breadth to our "internationalism" by including dances from countries not represented in the previous edition — Turkey, Ireland, and a Creole-African dance.

Much material has been added to the chapters on teaching, evaluation, and fundamentals. This expansion includes additional hints for students and teachers, sample objective questions for the testing of knowledge, and diagrams of formations used in folk dances. New to this edition are Styling Notes for most of the dances. These notes will enable the student to develop the individual nationality characteristics which lead to insight into the feelings and meanings of folk dance. Where possible, the Styling Notes include teaching hints, and sometimes interesting dance variations. A chapter has been added on How to Use the Book in order to help the reader use the dance descriptions and Rhythmic Learning Cues more effectively. Careful study of this chapter is important to both the teacher and student. In several places we have worked out a more effective organization of the materials, making the information easier to find, such as listing the dances in the Table of Contents as well as in the Classified Index. In summary, in this second edition we have up-graded and expanded the material in order to make the book easier to use in the teaching and learning of folk dances.

In our annual East Tennessee State University Fall Folk Dance Workshops and The Tennessee Octoberfest Folk Dance Camps, we have had wonderful experiences and have learned many dances. We must thank such well-known dance teachers as Vyts Beliajus, Dick Crum, Andor Czompo, Mel Diamond, David Henry, Bora Özkök, and Ken Spear. We are deeply indebted to Mary Ann Herman who has taught many years at our workshops and camps. Mary Ann and Michael Herman, recognized as authorities throughout the folk dance world, teach folk dances in New York City, at workshops in other countries, and at their summer-long Maine Folk Dance Camp. Many others have been our mentors, but special credit must go to Ken Warren and Helen Watson of Tennessee, M. G. Karsner and Ethel Capps of Kentucky, and Emery Butler of North Carolina.

The authors wish to express their deepest appreciation to William H. Cook, Marie Coward Blackwell, Jane Edgy, Naomi Hammons, Mary Kathryn Deaton, and Audrey Kaiman for their diligent work and assistance in completing the editions of this book.

# Chapter 1

## *Folk Dancing Past and Present*

Folk dancing is the oldest form of dance. It has been a basic part of culture as far back as historians and archaeologists can find records of man. Dance reflected the whole of man's life. The emotions and activities of work, worship, war, sowing, harvesting, courtship, and marriage were all represented in the movements of dance. Music and dance were so close that they were one, and it is only in the past few centuries of man's long history that these have been separated.

Dancing can be defined as the expression of feeling through rhythmic movement. Dance, therefore, is a form of communication, a way of speaking. Folk dancing is traditional dancing—the dancing which originated or was used among the people of a particular cultural area or geographic region, and has been handed down from one generation to another like other folk arts, such as folk songs and folk tales. Thus **folk dancing** can be defined as expressing oneself through rhythmically patterned movements, the style of which is determined by regional tradition.

Scholars who specialize in the study of folk dance find a fascinating history in exploring the rich heritage of folk dance that the ages have left us. In their research they may find several interpretations of one dance. Passing from one generation to the next and from one region to another, folk dances have taken on many variations, while at the same time the similarities can often be traced. The study of the design and color of folk costumes, or an analysis of folk dances in order to try to determine original sources and original purposes, or to see how folk dancing is an expression of the life, the history, the psychology of a people, and a basic part of their culture—all this makes for fascinating research and study.

Today, however, most people are interested in folk dancing because of its recreational values. Until recent years, the dancing of their traditional dances was one of the basic recreational activities of most people throughout the world. Even today this is still true in the rural areas of many countries, where everyone dances at wedding celebrations, family gatherings, and other festive occasions. As one travels through various countries, he finds that folk dancing is still very much a part of the lives of many peoples of the world.

Folk dancing came to our shores through several sources. Our own American square dancing and New England contra dancing have an old and respectable history, being derived from the dances that our colonial forefathers brought with them from the British Isles. In many instances immigrants from other countries brought their dances with them, and today, where there are good-sized enclaves of relatively recent immigrants, one finds national folk dances at every feast and celebration. Americans of older vintage, who have otherwise lost or forgotten their folk dance heritage, have learned or renewed their interest in their folk culture from these more recent Americans. Many other dances have been introduced by travelers and scholars who have learned the dances abroad.

Folk dancing is an integral part of the school program and has been included in the physical education curriculum since around the turn of the present century. Ann Barr and Elizabeth Burchenal are given credit by most historians as being the first to introduce folk dance to the schools in the United States. Today some curriculum experts recommend that for the lower elementary grades as much as 45 per cent of the physical education program should be devoted to a combination of singing games, creative movements, movement exploration, and folk dance, while in the upper elementary grades 25 per cent of the physical education class time for girls and 10 per cent for boys should be spent in the area of dance. They also recommend that one third of the physical education curriculum for high school girls should be devoted to dance and one tenth for boys. Dance now has an important place in the college curriculum, where one can find courses in folk, modern, social, square, ethnic, and tap dance. In some states all future teachers of physical education, both men and women, are required to study methods of teaching folk dance in order to meet certification requirements. Folk dance is an integral part of the curriculum because of the many ways in which it contributes to the broader objectives of education as well as physical education; therefore, practically every student in the U.S.A. is taught folk dance at some time during his school career.

Folk dancing in the United States today provides an important recreational activity outside of the school walls or campus. Many thousands of American adults are folk dancing every night of the week. Although some of these dancers are the recent immigrants, many more are members of folk dance clubs who meet regularly to enjoy the fun and fellowship of folk dancing. In some of our large cities it is possible to attend a different folk dance group every night for several weeks, and not repeat oneself. All during the year, folk dance weekends and week-long sessions are held at various interesting, scenic, and picturesque places. Colleges and universities sponsor many folk dance workshops and festivals. Nationally-known teachers of folk dancing, often of European origin, travel from group to group demonstrating new dances they have found as a result of their research, or helping beginners acquire dance skills. Folk dancing has grown enormously in the past 15 or 20 years, so that now it certainly must rank as one of the seven lively arts.

Why do we continue to do the dances of other peoples, countries, or periods of history? Folk dancing is:

1. A lot of fun.
2. A way to meet and be with other people.
3. A means of expressing oneself to music.
4. A good form of exercise.
5. A way to develop interest in and to understand other cultures or nations.
6. A way to release pent-up emotions.
7. An aid in improving coordination, agility, and balance.
8. A means of developing interest in other types of dancing.

Folk dancing can be done anywhere and by anyone. All that is necessary is to have some type of musical accompaniment, a level place, and interested people. The dances can be performed indoors or outdoors, with or without partners, by the highly skilled or non-skilled, by the old or young, and by all classes of people.

# Chapter 2

## Teaching Folk Dance

Folk dancing is an art which must be learned in order to enjoy it to its fullest. This means that good teaching is required. The learning process can be made most efficient, and enjoyment can be attained more readily where there is good teaching. Basic to success in teaching folk dance is a clear picture in the instructor's mind of the facilities, equipment, methods, and procedures which will aid him in achieving his goals.

### FACILITIES AND EQUIPMENT

The ideal room for dancing is well ventilated and has good acoustics, adequate lighting and heating, and sufficient floor space. Too small a space inhibits movement, while too large a space leads to acoustical problems. The dance floor should be smooth and clean. A slippery floor is both dangerous and uncomfortable to dance on, while a sticky dirty floor will not only inhibit smooth dancing but will be aesthetically displeasing.

Folk dance music formerly was supplied by the teacher or by an accompanist at a piano in one corner of the room. In the last 15 or 20 years, however, a wealth of excellent folk dance records have appeared, and they have become the standard musical accompaniment. (See page 125 for a list of dealers in folk dance records.) The record player purchased is frequently a compromise between price and versatility; however, such features as a variable-speed turntable, microphone, manual pickup arm, three-speed switching, and tone and volume controls, are all highly desirable. Probably most important is the variable-speed control which permits slowing the music for teaching purposes. A microphone which plugs into the record player is almost imperative when working with large groups. Changing the needle when necessary, keeping the records clean and carefully stored to reduce scratching, allowing only one person to use the record player and handle the records, saving old records for students to use for practice, getting the library to buy records, and arranging a regular system for setting up for class—all these make for good teaching and/or reduce equipment breakdowns.

### PLANNING THE MATERIAL

With equipment and room at hand, the teacher is ready to plan the lessons. Some suggestions follow:

1. Plan to work from easy to more difficult dances. Many of the easier dances are based on the walk or dance step, and this provides a reasonable starting point for beginners.
2. As proficiency develops, advanced dances with more complex dance steps such as the waltz and the polka can be introduced.
3. Plan to incorporate variety in formations, positions, steps, change-of-pace, types of dances, and use of mixer and novelty dances.
4. A typical daily lesson plan begins with a review of some previously learned dances, continues with the presentation of new material, and ends with a practice session on the new material.
5. Plan so that the desired objectives can be attained:

**Skill objectives**
a. To develop the ability to perform a broad range of steps and dances.
b. To dance rhythmically.
c. To dance so that timing, phrasing, and patterns are accurate.
d. To develop styling based on nationality characteristics and some individual polish.
e. To develop enough skill to enjoy the dance.

**Knowledge objectives**
a. To know steps, positions, formations, and dance patterns.
b. To know the nationality of various dances.
c. To know the history of dancing.
d. To know the story or legend associated with particular dances.
e. To understand the place of folk dancing in the folk arts.

**Social objectives**
a. To get acquainted with others.
b. To have fun.

6. The cardinal rule in planning, however, is to remain flexible. Classes vary and thus the plans must vary. Faced with a class composed mostly of young boys, the teacher will find a great deal of resistance to couple dances in which many of the boys are required to dance the part of a girl. An occasional class seems to be made up almost entirely of students with minimal rhythmic ability. The skilled teacher has faced such problems in the past and has developed the flexibility required to meet such situations. The teacher-in-training needs to be able to recognize such problems and to realize that plans can be changed, sequences modified, dances simplified, music slowed, parts broken down into smaller units, and so on.

## PREPARATION

Before attempting to teach a dance the teacher himself must be thoroughly familiar with the dance. Good teaching is basically the result of adequate preparation. The instructor must know the basic steps and the sequences of the pattern. He must be familiar with the music on the record he plans to use. He should be able to demonstrate the dance accurately, or have a good substitute to help him demonstrate it.

Both the teacher-in-training who must learn dances to teach and the experienced teacher who must broaden his range of materials will be constantly learning new dances. The dances in Chapters 6 and 7 are written to facilitate and simplify learning. Most teachers will find that they have no difficulty in learning these dances, even though they have never seen some of them performed.

The following steps are suggested as a method for learning or preparing to teach a folk dance:

1. Read over the dance and listen to the music at least one time.
2. Be sure that you can do the basic steps which are included in the dance before you try to learn the specific dance.
3. Walk through the dance. (Do this by parts if the dance is a long or difficult one.)
4. Learn the cues so that you can say them to yourself.
5. Listen to the music again, tap out the beat, work out the introduction, rhythm and timing.
6. Practice saying the Rhythmic Learning Cues to the music.
7. Try to perform the dance to the music. If the music seems too fast, adjust the turntable to a slower speed.
8. Listen to the phrasing of the music. Note the "highs and lows" of the music. Try to dance to the phrasing of music rather than counting 1, 2, 3, 4, . . . 8, etc. Get the feeling of the beat and rhythm. The cues and your footwork should correspond to the music.
9. Now try the dance at the correct speed.
10. If you have trouble with part of a dance, walk through this part over and over until you have the pattern fixed in your mind. Try it with the music again. Continue to practice until you can execute the pattern rhythmically and acquire a feeling of enjoyment. Overlearning a dance is necessary to develop the self-confidence that leads to good teaching.

The above list of suggestions can be given to students as a study guide in order to help them learn assigned material. In this case the teacher may want to add such suggestions as: "Watch the demonstration closely," "Listen to the instructor as the learning cues are called out," "Be earnest, enthusiastic, cooperative, and relaxed," etc.

## TEACHING A DANCE

There is no one method of teaching that fits all occasions or teachers; however, the basic principles and methods used by all good teachers apply to the teaching of folk dance. Each teacher after analyzing the situation will have to decide on the most appropriate method to use for teaching his particular group. For a recreational program the main objectives may be fun, satisfaction, and activity; therefore, some of the details of teaching techniques can be reduced. In the school situation, the student will be expected to acquire specific knowledges and skills, and will be evaluated in terms of his achievement. Because of this the teacher may need to give more time to teaching methods.

The experienced teacher has long since developed his own adaptations of general teaching methods. The teacher-in-training, with as yet little experience or opportunity to develop his own tried and true methods, needs a guide or model for his initial teaching. The following procedure is suggested for teaching a specific dance:

1. Have the students sit in a group close to the music. Give the name of the dance and its nationality. Tell something about the country, its people, and about the dance—especially if the dance tells a story.
2. Play the music. Have the class listen and then tap out the beat. (The volume of the record player should be adjusted so that it is at the proper level for listening.)
3. Demonstrate the dance. When necessary use the better students to help with the demonstrations. Go through the pattern twice at the correct tempo.
4. Have the class move into the designated formation and assume the position for the dance. The teacher can stand between the record player and the class, which places him near the music and in a favorable teaching position. In teaching single-circle dances, the teacher may join in the circle, the better to be seen and heard.
5. Teach the first part.
   a. Break long or advanced dances into parts. Always use the largest "teachable whole" suitable for the group. Try to use natural breaks —as a part, verse, chorus. Also note the phrasing of the music.
   b. Have the class walk through the pattern as you call out the rhythmic cues. The cues should be called out slowly at first, and then at correct tempo as soon as possible. (Further explanation and demonstration of a part are not necessary unless the group seems to be having difficulty. Use as few words as possible to get the class "into the dance." The class is already in the desired formation and position at this point so its members should become active as the teacher begins to talk.)
   c. Have the class try this part with the music while the teacher is calling out the rhythmic cues. Call the cues slightly in advance of the movement. Adjust the speed of the turntable so that most of the students can perform the steps in time with the music, and control the volume of the music so that the cues can be heard.
6. After the class has danced the first part, teach the second part by having the learners walk through it as the cues are given.
7. Have the class dance the first and second parts consecutively with the music and the rhythmic cues.
8. Continue in this manner until all parts have been taught.
9. After the last part has been walked through, have the class walk through the entire pattern with rhythmic cues being given in proper tempo.
10. Finally, have the class try the complete pattern with the music and the rhythmic cues. As the dance is learned, cut down on the use of cues, adjust the turntable to the correct speed, and increase the volume of the music.

## HINTS FOR THE TEACHER

1. Select short and easy non-partner or novelty dances at first so that all members of the class can participate and develop a feeling of accomplishment.
2. Familiarize yourself with the equipment, especially the record player.
3. Before introducing a difficult dance, it often helps to work through the dance with a small group.
4. Never try to teach until there is absolute quiet and attention.
5. The use of the blackboard can be very helpful in teaching dance names, nationalities, steps, and even diagrams of dance patterns.
6. The voice should be clear, pleasant, and distinct, loud enough to be heard. Needless to say, pronounciation should be correct.
7. The teacher's enthusiasm for dancing and sense of humor shows that he is a part of the group and enjoys the activity
8. Be sure that all members of the class are in position to see the demonstration.
9. Remember that students learn first through the eyes, next through the ears.
10. *Know* your dance, and *know* what you are doing.
11. Say what you are doing rather than how many times, e.g., "cross, side, back, side," instead of, "1, 2, 3, 4."
12. Use music *with* steps as much as possible. Minimize walk-throughs.

13. Do not waste time by talking through the dance. Have students "move" as you talk. Combine ACTION with your words.
14. Have students change partners frequently.
15. Spend practically all the class time teaching the group, not individuals. Give the individual help after the majority of the class has learned the dance.
16. Sometimes teaching a difficult dance can be made simpler by breaking the class up into small groups for learning and practice, with the teacher moving from group to group giving help.
17. Sometimes the most difficult part of a dance should be taught first since one learns "first" things better.
18. Teachers should feel free to simplify dances when working with little children, handicapped students, etc.
19. Some instructors advise teachers not to dance with the class while teaching.
20. Most dance teachers are guilty of talking too much and teaching too slowly. Usually, a group is capable of learning much faster than is generally thought possible.
21. After the dance has been learned, have the class do the dance again for satisfaction and fun, leaving the students with a feeling of accomplishment.
22. Frequent reviews of dances permit more learning and lead to freer self-expression and enjoyment.
23. In a recreational group, in order to maintain a relaxed atmosphere, one might permit frequent periods of conversation during the teaching sessions. Thus the social aspect of dance is enhanced.
24. For many dances, records that are popular and appropriate can be substituted in place of the one listed in this book. In some cases one can find interesting records that fit certain dances with specific rhythms and patterns, such as waltzes, schottisches, polkas, etc. Record companies frequently produce new arrangements. Don't hesitate to experiment with new records. Encourage students to try dance patterns to current hit records.

## HINTS FOR THE STUDENT

1. Be comfortable. Wear comfortable shoes and clean clothes that do not restrict movement. Use a deodorant.
2. Be considerate. Cooperate with and help your partner or neighbors. Keep your enthusiasm to a reasonable level. Control your arms and legs. Maintain the pattern and rhythm. Good manners are always appropriate.
3. Be relaxed. Tension results mostly from being unsure of oneself. Practice and learn the dances well so that you can relax and enjoy yourself.
4. Be balanced. With a partner, balance pull against pull. Be ready to move in the right direction; this is accomplished by always having the free foot poised and ready. When your weight is on both feet, you cannot be ready to move rhythmically and on time. Stand tall, easy, and ready.
5. Be positive. Everyone can learn to dance and enjoy folk dancing. With a positive attitude learning is easier and confidence develops quickly.
6. Be responsive. Try to feel the beat and dynamics. Memorizing a pattern and walking through it does not mean you are dancing. Dancing is expressing yourself through movements in time with the music. The dynamics of the music — the highs and lows — the intensity — the mood — all should be reflected in your dancing.

# Chapter 3

## Evaluation in Folk Dance

How much skill and knowledge should a folk dancer have? Enough to enjoy performing the dance!

When folk dances are taught as a part of a recreational program, success may be evaluated solely in terms of fun or satisfaction. If the folk dances are taught in a class as part of a school program for which credit is recorded, periodic evaluations at given intervals have to be made in terms of the desired educational objectives.

The **evaluation of skill** in folk dancing is based on a subjective estimate of the dancer's performance in the form of a **rating**. There are no objective folk dance skill tests such as the wall volley which can be used as one aspect of measurement in activities like volleyball, badminton, and tennis; therefore, the folk dance teacher must rely on ratings which he tries to make as valid, reliable, and objective as possible.

The first step in rating should be to determine specifically what is to be measured. This can be done "as a whole" by observing both the general knowledge and skill of the student as he performs. The measurement can be made more specific by selecting a basic step such as the waltz, and rating the student as he does either a series of waltz steps accompanied by waltz music or a dance which incorporates the waltz as one of its basic steps.

Next, the rating categories must be selected and clearly defined. The most commonly used categories are good, average, and poor; these can be recorded +, ✔, −, or 3, 2, 1. These categories may be defined as follows:

The *good* dancer (+ or 3) knows the patterns and steps, performs the dance skillfully and rhythmically, and he feels or expresses the spirit of the dance.

The *average* dancer (✔ or 2) learns the dance well enough to execute the pattern, makes corrections when he realizes that he has made a mistake, and seems to enjoy the dance.

The *poor* dancer (− or 1) makes errors in the pattern and probably is not able to correct his errors by watching others; he does not move rhythmically nor have the feeling of the dance.

Some teachers may prefer to use five rating categories such as excellent, very good, good, fair, and poor.

A suggested procedure to use is:

1. Assign each student a number which he wears to class regularly. This makes ratings more objective and helps save time. (The student can make his own number. It must be large enough to be read easily.)
2. Design a rating sheet.
3. Pick out and record ratings for the good (+) and poor (−) dancers while the students are performing. After class, record a "✔" for the others who were present.
4. Arrange a periodic "skill test day"—a class meeting set aside for students to demonstrate their skills.
5. Determine the final skill grade by averaging the several ratings.

Students and teachers-in-training should have an opportunity to rate each other. The more experience and training a rater has, the more valid and reliable his rating will be. The student's rating can be combined or compared with the teacher's rating in order to avoid the so-called "halo effect." (Certain influences may lower the validity of a rating—politeness, popularity, friendship, etc.) Another important benefit is that students will be better dancers if they understand specifically what is expected of them, and in the process of rating others they will become aware of what it takes to be a good dancer. Using some modification of the Lapp Rating Technique (which can be found in physical education test and measurement books), students can participate in the rating of class members. Each is given a rating sheet designed for this purpose. Figure 1 illustrates such a class rating sheet for a hypothetical class of 20.

---

**CLASS RATING SHEET**

(Modification of the Lapp Rating Technique)

From your own observation of, or experience of dancing with the members of the class, select the 4 best dancers and the 4 poorest dancers.

Indicate your rating by placing next to the number of the student a + (plus) for the best dancers, and a − (minus) for the poorest dancers.

As you rate, think of these descriptions:

A good dancer knows the patterns and steps, performs the dance skillfully and rhythmically, and he feels or expresses the spirit of the dance.

A poor dancer makes errors in the pattern and probably is not able to correct his errors by watching others, and he does not move rhythmically nor have the feeling of the dance.

| | |
|---|---|
| 1. | 11. |
| 2. − | 12. − |
| 3. | 13. |
| 4. − | 14. |
| 5. | 15. |
| 6. + | 16. + |
| 7. | 17. |
| 8. | 18. |
| 9. + | 19. − |
| 10. | 20. + |

**Figure 1**

The teacher can tabulate the ratings, rank the class members according to the ratings, and even assign letter grades. Figures 2 and 3 illustrate such tabulations and show how the members of a class of twenty might rate each other's skill, their ranking, and the resulting letter grades which were assigned.

In addition to evaluating skill, **objective knowledge tests** can be constructed which are based on the dances, steps, formations, positions, nationalities, and other such information. Various types of questions can be used but the following seem to be particularly good in testing for this type of information: multiple choice questions for testing knowledge of basic folk dance steps; matching questions for checking information about the nationalities of dances; true-false statements for checking knowledge pertaining to the basic steps included in a dance, formation and position, and the identification of cues for dance patterns, names, and patterns of dances. See Figure 4 for sample test questions.

The progress of the **teacher-in-training** who is learning to teach folk dancing also needs to be evaluated. Such factors as the factual knowledge of folk

---

**TABULATION OF CLASS RATINGS**
6th Period Class

| POOR − | STUDENT NUMBER | GOOD + | SUMMARY SCORE (No. of +'s minus no. of −'s) |
|---|---|---|---|
| − | 1 | | −1 |
| − − − | 2 | | −3 |
| − − | 3 | + | −1 |
| − − − − − | 4 | | −5 |
| − − | 5 | + + | 0 |
| − | 6 | + + + + + + + + + + | +9 |
| | 7 | + | +1 |
| | 8 | | 0 |
| | 9 | + + + + | +4 |
| − − | 10 | | −2 |
| − | 11 | | −1 |
| − − − − − − − − − | 12 | | −9 |
| | 13 | + + | +2 |
| | 14 | | 0 |
| | 15 | | 0 |
| | 16 | + + + + + + + + + + + + + | +13 |
| − | 17 | + | 0 |
| | 18 | | 0 |
| − − − | 19 | + + + | 0 |
| − | 20 | + + + + | +3 |

**Figure 2**

---

**CLASS RANKING AND GRADE**
6th Period Class

| STUDENT NUMBER | SUMMARY SCORE | GRADE |
|---|---|---|
| 16 | +13 | A |
| 6 | + 9 | A− |
| 9 | + 4 | B |
| 20 | + 3 | B |
| 13 | + 2 | B |
| 7 | + 1 | C+ |
| 5 | 0 | C |
| 8 | 0 | C |
| 14 | 0 | C |
| 15 | 0 | C |
| 17 | 0 | C |
| 18 | 0 | C |
| 19 | 0 | C |
| 1 | − 1 | C− |
| 3 | − 1 | C− |
| 11 | − 1 | C− |
| 10 | − 2 | D |
| 2 | − 3 | D |
| 4 | − 5 | D− |
| 12 | − 9 | F |

**Figure 3**

dancing, practice teaching, and folk dance skills can all enter into the evaluation of the teacher-in-training. Learning about folk dancing requires wide reading of books and periodicals relating to folk dance, and the extent and depth of learning can often be evaluated by oral or written tests. The development of skill in folk dancing requires much practice and interest, and can be evaluated by means of ratings as mentioned above. Practice teaching makes an important contribution to the career of the teacher-in-training, and some careful thinking is necessary in this aspect of evaluation. Most instructors of student-teachers consider such factors as the student-teacher's preparation and knowledge of his materials, his demonstration of dances, his method of teaching, his appearance, poise, voice, and control of his class. Again, a three- or five-category rating scale can be used to rate the student on each of these factors as the instructor observes the practice teaching. A real help to student-teachers in developing validity and reliability in their own ratings is to rate each other on these and other factors, and to check their ratings against those of the experienced instructor.

Evaluating skill by both daily and periodic ratings and measuring knowledge with objective tests will provide both the student and the teacher with a real idea of a student's progress in learning folk dancing. Learning leads to enjoyment. Evaluation motivates students to become better dancers. The more a person enjoys folk dancing, the more often he will participate in it.

---

**SAMPLE QUESTIONS**

**I.  Fundamental Steps:**

MATCHING: Record the number of the description which matches the step.

(3)  1. Kick
(1)  2. Run
(4)  3. Slide

1. Rhythmical transfer of weight from one foot to the other but for a brief moment both feet are off the floor.
2. Step to the side, bringing other foot up to it and transfer weight.
3. With weight on one foot, thrust the other foot in the specified direction.
4. Step to the side and quickly bring up the other foot and shift weight to it.

MULTIPLE CHOICE: Select the correct answer and record the number in the blank.

(4)  1. Polka
1. Hop, step, hop, step.
2. Step, together, step, hop.
3. Step, step, hop.
4. Hop, step, close, step.

(2)  2. Waltz
1. Step, slide-by, step.
2. Step, step, close.
3. Step, together, step, close.
4. Step, close, step.

(1)  3. Two-step
1. Step, together, step, pause.
2. Step, step, pause.
3. Step, step, together, pause.
4. Step, together, step.

**II.  Positions:**

MATCHING: Record the number of the description which matches the position.

(1)  1. Barrel
(4)  2. V-Position
(3)  3. Open

1. Hands clasped with neighbor's and held forward at shoulder level, but with arms rounded.
2. Stand side-by-side, right hands are joined and left hands are joined.
3. Stand side-by-side, holding inside hands.
4. Arms are held straight down, hands clasped with neighbor's about hip level.

MULTIPLE CHOICE: Select the correct answer and record the number in the blank.

(2)  1. Side-by-side, facing same direction. Man's right arm around behind lady's waist. Her left hand on his right shoulder.
1. Varsovienne position
2. Schottische position
3. Promenade position
4. Banjo position

(2)  2. Side-by-side, facing same direction. His right arm behind her, holding her right hand above her right shoulder.
1. Shoulder-waist position
2. Varsovienne position
3. Banjo position
4. Two-hand position

**III.  Dances:**

MATCHING: Record the number of the dance which matches the phrase.

(6)  1. Represents a hammer and anvil
(4)  2. Aunt Esther's White Horse
(1)  3. Water, Water
(2)  4. Peddler's Pack

1. Mayim
2. Korobushka
3. Java
4. Tant' Hessie

5. Raksi Jaak
6. Kalvelis

MULTIPLE CHOICE: Select the dance that corresponds with the rhythmical cues.

(3)  1. Strut, 2, 3, 4. Rock forward, backward, forward, backward. Repeat.
Step, close, cross, and step, close, cross. Turn 2, 3, 4. Repeat.
1. Good Old Days
2. Twelfth Street Rag
3. Walkin' & Whistlin'
4. Java

(3)  2. Schottische to the right, schottische to the left. Skate, skate, skate, skate.
1. American Schottische
2. Korobushka
3. Ostende
4. Savila Se Bela Loza

**Figure 4**

# Chapter 4

## *Folk Dance Fundamentals*

Everyone needs to know some basic skills in order to develop the ability and confidence which characterize a good dancer.

The first section of this chapter will explain what to do with the feet, the next section describes what to do with the hands, and the last section tells what to do with the people.

### BASIC FOLK DANCE STEPS
### or What to Do With the Feet

#### THE STEP

The basic movement in folk dancing is walking. In fact, one way to look at all the various folk dance steps used is to think of these as variations and combinations of the basic walking step. Ordinary walking is done on the heels. The dance walk differs mainly in that one is up on the balls of the feet. This permits better balance and rhythm and allows the dancer to move more freely.

**Step.** Place one foot on the floor, and shift weight to it. This is the fundamental unit of dance. One can step on the ball of the foot, the heel, or the entire foot depending on the ethnic nature of the dance. According to the dance pattern, a dancer can take one step or several steps.

**Dance Walk.** Technically, we can describe the dance walk as a locomotor movement in any horizontal direction, alternating the feet rhythmically, and keeping the weight of the body supported (usually up on the balls of the feet) on one foot which remains in contact with the floor until the other foot contacts the floor and takes the weight.

Let us look at some variations of the *step or dance walk*. The simplest are variations which are based on one *step*.

### Variations on One Step

**Run.** Like the walk, but with more elevation and for just a moment both feet are off the floor.

**Leap.** A transfer of weight from one foot to the other by springing higher off the floor than in the run and for a longer moment.

**Hop.** Lightly springing off the floor from one foot and landing on the same foot.

**Jump.** Springing off the floor, using both feet together.

**Bounce.** Not entirely springing off the floor, but just getting the heels off.

**Touch.** With weight on one foot, bring the ball (or heel) of the other foot lightly in contact with the floor.

**Point.** With weight on one foot, touch the other toe (sometimes the heel) to the floor in any direction.

**Kick.** With weight on one foot, vigorously thrust the other foot in any direction.

**Swing.** With weight on one foot, gently thrust the other foot in any direction, in a pendulum-like movement.

**Brush.** With weight on one foot, touch the floor lightly with the ball of the other foot while kicking.

**Pivot.** With weight on one foot, turn quickly and smoothly to face the opposite direction (sometimes completely around depending on the dance).

**Stamp.** Hit the floor vigorously with the foot (sometimes just the heel).

**Strut.** Exaggerating the knee-bends on the off-beat makes the walk into a strut.

### Variations or Combinations of Two Steps

**Step-close.** Step to one side with one foot, then bring the other foot up to it, and shift the weight.

**Slide.** Like the step-close, but a little more elevation and usually a little faster. (Called *slip-step* in English country dancing.) Step to the side and quickly bring up the other foot, shifting the weight to it.

**Sashay.** Like the slide, but more elevation. (Sometimes called *chassez*, or *chassé*.)

**Galop.** Like the shashay, but still more elevation.

**Step-touch.** Step (any direction), then lightly touch other foot to the floor.

**Step-draw.** Step to one side, then lightly drag up the other foot, and shift weight.

**Step-swing.** Step on one foot, and at the same time swing the other.

**Step-hop.** Step on one foot, then hop on it.

**Hop-point.** Hop on one foot, at the same time point the other.

**Heel and toe.** Touch one heel to the floor, then the toe of the same foot.

**Buzz.** One foot leads continually and the other foot pushes. (This step often looks like limping or like a child on his scooter.) This is done as a series of several steps. A circle of dancers might do 6 or 8 buzz-steps to the left (right foot leading and left foot pushing) or to the right (left foot leading, and right pushing).

**Buzz-step Swing.** Couples pivot or turn in place with the leading foot moving in a little circle around which the two dancers revolve by pushing with the other foot. If the two dancers will place their right feet together, outside-of-foot adjacent to outside-of-foot, and in banjo (p. 13) position, lean slightly away from each other, then start the buzz-step swing, the momentum attained as they revolve around each other can be considerable.

**Chug.** Moving sideways, fall on the lead foot (left foot, if moving left, etc.) while the trailing foot first pushes, then closes. This is often done in a series, (fall, push, fall, push, fall, push, fall), then reversing footwork back to original position. To give the step flavor and style, the trailing foot can push and twist a little. Then there is another **Chug** which involves moving one or both feet across the floor. With weight on that foot (or feet) and maintaining contact with the floor, one makes a short, sharp movement of an inch or two forward (or backward, as required).

## Variations and Combinations of Three or More Steps

**Two-step.** Step forward on one foot, bring up and shift weight to the trailing foot, step forward on the lead foot, and pause. Usually done as a series repeating the action and alternating the lead foot. (Cue: left, close, left, pause; right, close, right, pause, etc.)

**Pas-de-Bas.** (Pronounced: PAH-dee-bah.) Quickly and with considerable elevation, leap to one side,

bring the trailing foot across in front of the lead foot and briefly step on toe of the trailing foot, then quickly step on the lead foot in place. In some dances done as a series, first to one side, then the other. (Cue: leap, step, step.)

**Threes or Triplets.** 3 quick steps almost in place, alternating feet (R-L-R or L-R-L), sometimes a little more emphasis on the first of the three steps. (Cue: step-step-step.)

**Waltz.** Step forward on lead foot, bring the other foot out to the side or forward, then close the lead foot to the trailing foot. Each sequence of three steps starts with alternating feet (R, L, R; L, R, L; etc.). Usually the waltz is done smoothly and lightly. (Cue: step, step, close.)

**Waltz-Balance.** Step forward (or backward) on one foot, step on the trailing foot beside the lead foot while rising up on the balls of both feet, step again in place on the lead foot. (Cue: step, rise, step.)

**Polka.** Quite similar to the two-step, but begins with a hop. Hop quickly on one foot, step the other foot forward, close free foot to it and shift weight, then step again. (Cue: hop, step, close, step.)

**Schottische.** (Pronounced: SHAH-tish.) Again like the two-step, but ends with a hop. Step on lead foot, close other foot to it and shift weight, step on lead foot again and hop. (Cue: step, close, step, hop.) Or, in some dances, three steps forward and hop on the last step. (Cue: step, step, step, hop; or run, run, run, hop.)

**Grapevine.** Step one foot across the other foot, step free foot to the side, then step the first foot behind the other foot, and step to the side. This is often done with some elevation. (Cue: cross, step, behind, step.)

**Mazurka.** Basically, step, step, hop. Or step, close, hop. In one variation of this (called **Varsouvianna**) sweep one foot back across the other, then step diagonally forward on it, and close with the other foot. The same foot always leads in a series of steps. (Cue: sweep, step, close.)

In another variation (called **Varsovienne**), take 3 walking steps, then point the free foot, and pause. As a couple dances, the man often moves (crosses) the lady from one side to the other, while taking small steps. (Cue: step, step, step, point, pause.)

**Charleston.** Step forward on one foot, point the trailing foot forward. Then step back on this trailing foot. Point the lead foot backward. (Cue: step, point, step, point.)

Also see Glossary, p. 124.

## POSITIONS
### or What to Do With the Hands

Here are some of the typical folk dance arm and hand positions partners can use, and also some hand-holds used in non-partner dances.

In holding hands with a partner in a couple dance or a neighbor in a non-partner dance, men always turn their hands palms up. Ladies take the man's hand with their palms down. The exception to this is in a non-partner dance when several men, or several ladies, stand together — then one's right hand is turned palm up, and the left hand palm down.

In any of the partner-facing positions, each should lean the shoulders away from the other a little. This gives much better balance, especially in turns and swings.

**Open Position.** Partners stand side-by-side, facing same direction, lady on man's right, holding inside hands—the hands nearest each other.

**COUPLE DANCE POSITIONS**

**Promenade Position.** Also called **Skating** position. Partners side-by-side, facing same direction, lady on man's right. Right hands are joined, and left hands are joined, with his right arm over her left arm, about waist high.

**Closed Position.** Also called **Ballroom** position, or **Social Dance** position. Partners stand facing each other, the man with his right arm around the lady, his right hand firmly just under her shoulder blade. His left arm is somewhat extended and he holds her right hand in his left hand. Her left hand rests on his right shoulder. (In **Semi-closed** position partners are standing more side-by-side, so that his right side and her left side are adjacent.)

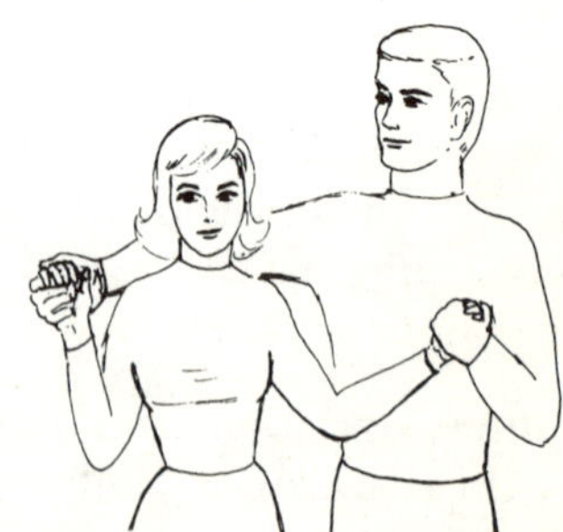

**Varsovienne Position.** (Pronounced: vahr-soo-vee-EHN.) Partners, side-by-side, facing same direction, lady on man's right. His right arm is behind her, holding her right hand above her right shoulder. His left hand holds her left hand about in front of his chest.

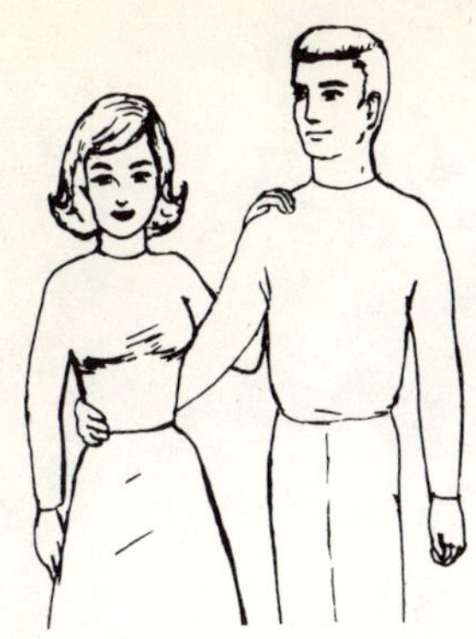

**Schottische Position.** (Pronounced: SHAH-tish.) Partners, side-by-side, facing same direction, lady on man's right. His right arm is around behind her, holding her waist. Her left hand rests on his right shoulder. His left hand and her right hand are free. (In the **Skater's** position, his left hand holds her left hand about in front of his chest.)

**Banjo Position.** Also called **Side** position or **Right Shoulder** position. Partners face, a little to the side of each other so that man's right side is adjacent to lady's right side. His right arm is around her waist. His left arm, elbow sharply bent, is at shoulder height. His left hand holds her right hand, her right arm is outstretched, her left hand rests on his right arm. This position is the one used for the Buzz-Step Swing. In the **Hungarian-Turn** position, both have right arms around the partner's waist, and both have left arms raised overhead.

**Shoulder-Waist Position.** Partners face. Man's arms are outstretched, with both hands holding lady's waist. Her hands are on his shoulders.

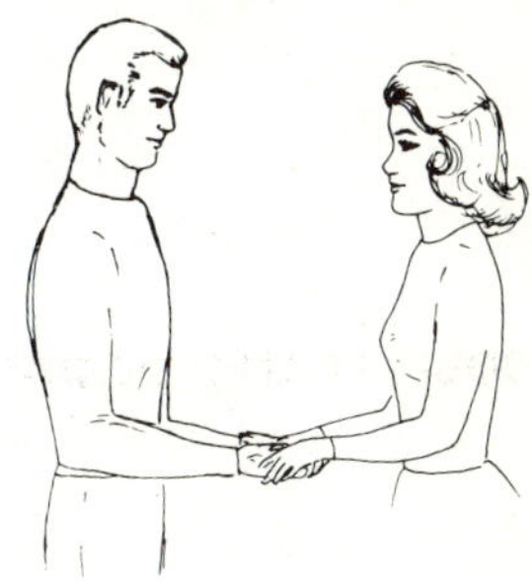

**Two-Hand Position.** Partners face, and hands are joined about waist high.

## LINE DANCE POSITIONS

**Some hand holds used in non-partner dances:**

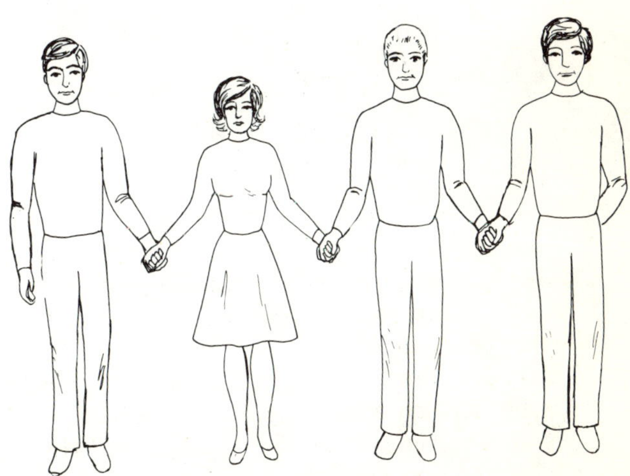

**Basic Position.** Arms are held down, not stiff, elbows bent a little, and hands are clasped with neighbors' at about waist level.

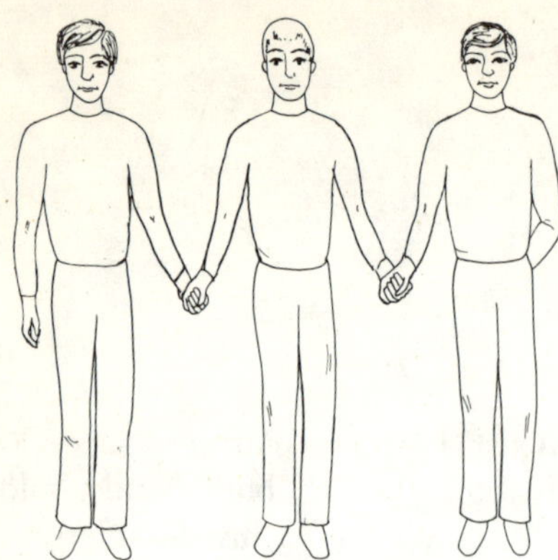

**V-Position.** Arms are held straight down, not stiff, hands clasped with neighbors' about hip level.

**W-Position.** Arms are bent at the elbows, hands are clasped with neighbors' about shoulder level, just a few inches forward of the shoulders. The **Barrel Position** is similar to the **W**-position, except that the hands are held about 10 or 12 inches forward of the shoulders. (It's called the Barrel Position because the arms are rounded as if each person were hugging a barrel to his chest.)

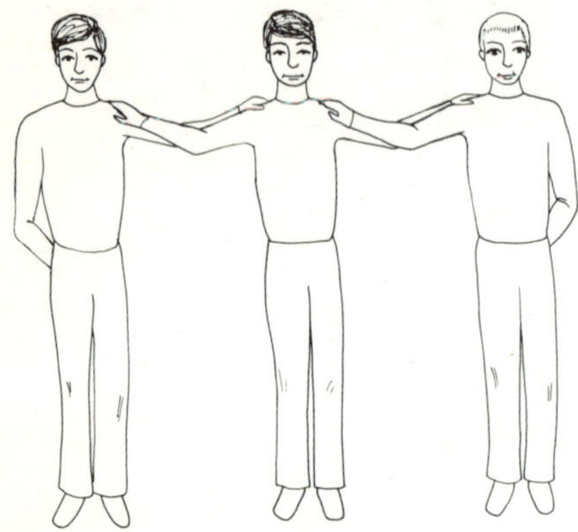

**Shoulder Position.** Arms up and outstretched to the sides, hands on the neighbors' shoulders closest to you. Hands must rest lightly, and not pull.

**Basket Holds.** Arms are outstretched, and hands are clasped with the persons on either side of your neighbors—your right hand clasps the left hand of the person to the right of your neighbor to your right, and your left hand clasps the right hand of the person to the left of the neighbor to your left. In a *Front Basket,* the arms and hands are in front of everyone, while in a *Back Basket,* arms and hands are held behind neighbors' backs.

**Arms-up position,** hands are clasped with neighbors' about head height.

## FORMATIONS
### or What to Do With the People

Arranging the dancers on the dance floor can be done in many ways. Here are some of the most typical ways.

Symbols    Man    Lady

**Free Formation.** Single dancers, couples, trios, or larger groups scatered freely all around the room.

**Line.** A file of dancers. Often facing the center of the room or CCW. Usually a line is short—4, 5, or 6 dancers.  Fig. 5.

**Figure 5**

**Single Circle, Broken.** A ring of dancers, but open so that one dancer, usually on the right end, is the leader.  Fig. 6.

**Figure 6**

**Single Circle, Closed.** A complete ring of dancers. Can be facing CW, CCW, or the center of the circle.  Fig. 7.

Partners in a closed single circle can be standing side-by-side, (all facing the center, and usually with the lady on right side of her partner); or partners can be facing each other (man facing CCW, lady CW).  Fig. 8.

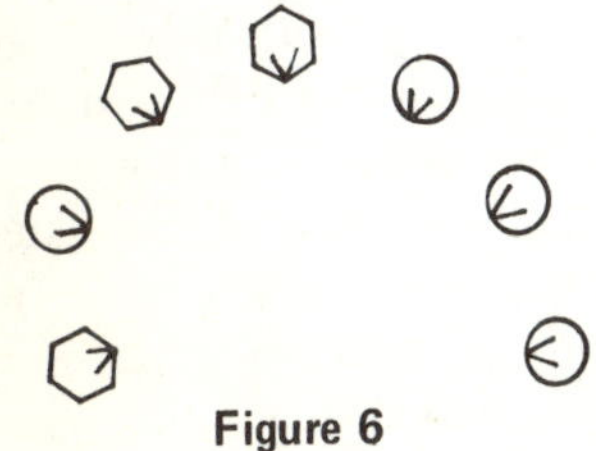

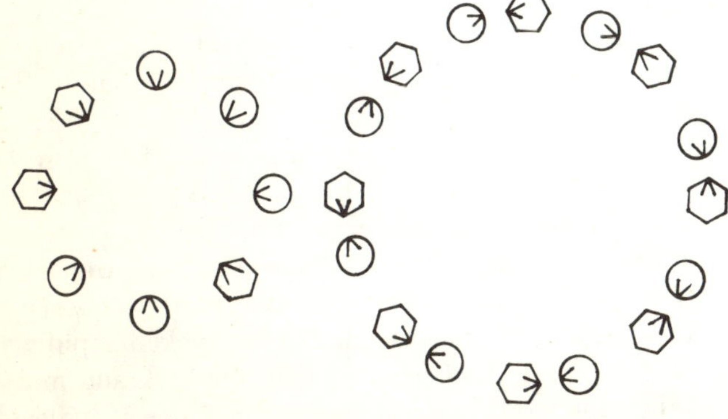

**Figure 7**        **Figure 8**

**Double Circle.** Almost always is a closed circle, and is composed of couples. Partners can be standing side-by-side (facing CCW), Fig. 9, partners can be facing each other (the men standing with their backs to the center of the room while their partners face the center) Fig. 10, or couples can face couples (one facing CW, the other CCW).

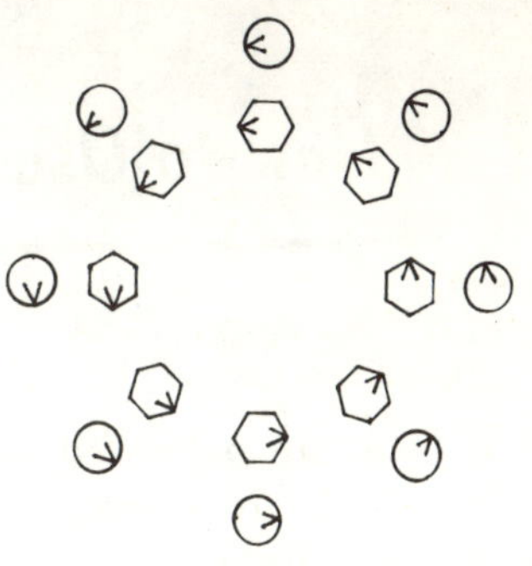

**Figure 9**

**Figure 10**

**Trio.** A group of three dancers, the center person usually being of opposite gender from the outside persons.

Many *other formations* are possible:

a circle of 2 couples facing 2 couples;

a circle of trios, or of trios facing trios;

a line of couples straight down the room, with all the men on one side and all the ladies on the other side (contra, or longways);

a square of four couples, each standing as if on one side of an 8-foot square.

groups of 2, 3, 4, 5, or 6 dancers all in lines which radiate from the center of the room, like the spokes of a wheel.

# Chapter 5

## *How to Use the Book*

The folk dances in this book are organized into two chapters: Chapter 6, Easy to Learn Dances, and Chapter 7, Moderately Easy to Learn Dances. Each chapter is then separated into three divisions, non-partner dances, couple dances, and dances for three or more people. Each dance is described step by step and then is summarized in rhythmical learning cues. We have tried to include everything the teacher and the student need in order to learn the dance, and have eliminated that which we find unimportant.

For instance, we have eliminated all references to musical notation and musical time signature, but have built the dance descriptions around a clear indication of the time and rhythm for each dance based on the Beat. We have found that few teachers, teachers-in-training, and students are familiar with the intricacies of musical notation and timing.

It seems to us, also, that the "folk" from whom folk dances originally came, had little or no knowledge of formal musical notation. In our experience with Southern Appalachian folk musicians and folk dancers, the entire process of folk music depended on learning the tunes "by ear," and all the dancing was done on the beat provided by the musicians. It is this process that we are using in the book — not so much for the sake of authenticity — but more because we think that the use of the beat makes folk dances easier to learn and easier to teach.

The **Beat** is the unit of music heard on the record that is most usually defined by the rhythm instruments — the drums, or the bass viol, etc. While the melody or tune may provide the phrases which define the sections or parts of the dance, the beat defines the tempo or speed of the dance movements, as well as the rhythms.

To learn a dance, one must first read and learn the descriptions of the dance steps. The next step is to listen closely to the music — and tap out the beat with the foot. With each dance description there is a **Timing and Rhythm** indicator designed to help tie together the dance steps and the music. Having learned the steps, and listened to the music to identify the beat, one can then proceed to dance the steps as fast as indicated by the Timing and Rhythm. For example, the Timing and Rhythm indicator for the dance "Alley Cat" (p. 19) calls for one dance step per beat, following a short three-note introduction on the record used. After listening to the record, and tapping out the beat, you can then step off the dance, one step per beat of music. A more specific outline of the procedure for learning a dance is found in the section on Preparation, page 4.

All of the dances in this book have relatively simple rhythms, and in every case the beat is readily identifiable on most of the records listed. There are, however, many dances with very complex rhythms and intricate accents. An excellent discussion of the beat and rhythmic patterning is found in the book *Folk Dance Progressions* by Miriam Lidster and Dorothy Tamburini (1965).

Unique and original in this book are the **Rhythmic Learning Cues** at the end of nearly every dance description. These cues provide the learner with a rhythmic summary of the important aspects of the dance, including timing, steps, directions, and other information to help the student over the rough spots. While the detailed description of the dance provides the basic framework for learning the entire pattern, the Rhythmic Learning Cues provide the brief and immediate memory aid that one needs as the music is playing. In the Cues all hyphenated words (e.g., step-behind, step-swing) should be spoken rapidly in order to keep the Cues with the footwork and music. When the word "and" is used in the Cues, it indicates a pause.

The dances which have been selected represent

the culture of twenty-three nations and involve most of the basic, fundamental steps. Many non-partner dances are included because very few of the folk dance classes in the school situation are made up of an equal number of fellows and girls. Some mixer type dances are included to give students an opportunity to get acquainted with others in the class and to dance with the better dancers. Several "novelty" dances which have been choreographed to recent catchy tunes and are fun to dance are also included. Teachers will find these novelty dances to be the favorite dances because the students are familiar with such music, which usually has a strong, easily recognizable beat, and they can let themselves go in this sort of rhythm. We have indicated some variations of the dances and encourage you to try these and other variations. One advantage in so doing is that the dancer can adapt or modify the pattern to meet his interest or skill level.

All the dances are described in material that is original in this book, and written so as to make learning as efficient as possible. The source of each dance is given if it has been clearly established. However, it is often difficult to name the specific individual who brought a dance to this country, or who might claim credit for popularizing a certain dance. Sources are sometimes vague and ambiguous, and this is especially so for those dances which have long been popular and well-loved.

Correctly pronouncing the names of the dances is not always easy, for few students or teachers of folk dance have so wide a background in foreign languages. We have tried to indicate the preferred pronounciation of the names of the dances. Each word is broken into appropriate syllables. The accented syllable is indicated by capital leters. The guttural German "ch" (as in Bach) is indicated by "kh", as in Kuma Echa (KOO-ma EH-kha). Other letters are pronounced as in English.

The following abbreviations are used in this book:

| | | | |
|---|---|---|---|
| L | left foot | diag | diagonally |
| R | right foot | Q | quick |
| CCW | counterclockwise | S | slow |
| CW | clockwise | O | outside foot |
| fwd | forward | I | inside foot |
| swd | sideward | var | variation |
| bwd | backward | ptnr | partner |
| LOD | line of direction | | |

Several tables and lists of dances are included in the **Appendix.** These will serve as a handy reference to both the student and teacher in selecting dances, locating them in the book, and in summarizing the dances according to nationality, basic steps, type, and difficulty rating. A list of books and periodicals, which may be used for additional reading or background material, is included in the Appendix as well as a list of record dealers from the various sections of the United States, who can supply records for the dances presented.

# Chapter 6

## Dance Patterns Easy to Learn

This chapter includes forty-six easy-to-learn dances. They are grouped according to the number of dancers involved in the dance — Non-Partner, Couple, More than Three. Each group is arranged alphabetically. You will note that some dances can be placed in more than one category. Many of these dances are based on the walking step; however, there is a variety of all the basic steps. The dances in each category are listed below.

### NON-PARTNER DANCES



### COUPLE AND MIXER DANCES



### DANCES FOR THREE OR MORE

# ALLEY CAT



A novelty dance, set to a recent American hit record. Dottie Dicks of the Methodist Recreation Lab in Leesburg, Florida, and Marie Armstrong of Port Richie, Florida, originated the dance.

**Records:** ATCO 45-6226; Columbia CL 2500.

**Steps:** Touch, step, jump.

**Formation:** No partners, free formation. For learning, everyone can face the same direction.

**Timing and Rhythm:** One beat per step (brief 3-note introduction on A 45-6226).

**PATTERN:**

PART I:    Touch R sideward to right, then bring it back and touch alongside L, touch R out to side again, then bring it back and step on it.

Repeat Part I, beginning L.

PART II:    Touch R backwards, then touch R beside L, touch R backward again, then bring it back and step on it.

Repeat Part II, beginning L.

PART III:    Raise R knee up in front of L knee, and repeat. Then raise L knee up twice. Then raise R knee once, L knee once.

PART IV:    Clap your hands once and jump, making a quarter turn to own right.

*Repeat the dance, making a quarter turn with each repetition, facing a different wall of the room with each quarter turn.*

**RHYTHMIC LEARNING CUES:**

I:    *(Swd)*    
R   R   R   R  
Touch, touch, touch, step.

"    
L   L   L   L  
Touch, touch, touch, step.

II:    *(Bwd)*    
R   R   R   R  
Touch, touch, touch, step.

"    
L   L   L   L  
Touch, touch, touch, step.

III:    *(In place)*    
R   R   L   L  
Knee, knee; knee, knee.

"    
R   L  
Knee, knee.

IV:    *(Turn right)*    Clap, and jump.

**AS A COUPLE DANCE:** Partners, facing each other and starting on opposite or same feet, end with a double jump so as to continue facing partner.

**Styling:** As in many novelty dances, use jazz and rock movements — let yourself go!

# AMOS MOSES

AMERICAN

A novelty dance set to a recent American hit record by Jerry Reed. Described as learned from "Stew" Shacklette, of Louisville, Kentucky.

Record:  RCA 447-0896.

**Steps:**  Touch, step.

**Formation:**  No partners, free formation. For learning, everyone can face the same direction.

**Timing & Rhythm:**  One beat per step (brief 4-note introduction on RCA 447-0896).

### PATTERN:

PART I:    Touch R sideward to right, then bring it back and step on R beside L.
Touch L sideward to left, then step on L beside R.

Repeat Part I, again beginning R.

PART II:    Step forward on R (in the direction you are facing), step on L behind R while making almost a quarter turn to the left, step sideward to the right on R then pivoting on R to make a half turn to the right, step sideward to the left on L.

*Repeat the dance, making a quarter turn with each repetition, facing a different wall of the room with each quarter turn.*

### RHYTHMIC LEARNING CUES:

            R    R    L    L
I:        (*Swd*)    Touch, step, touch, step.

            R    R    L    L
          Touch, step, touch, step.

            R    L    R    L
II:        (*Fwd*)    Forward, behind, pivot, step.

**Styling:**  The music is rock and roll — and the dance is done with rock movements of the shoulders, torso and hips.

# APAT-APAT

Pronounced: AH-paht AH-paht

This is one of the popular dances introduced by Francisca Aquino, the noted Philippine dance authority.

Record: Folk Dancer MH2022.

**Step:** Walking step.

**Formation:** Partners, double circle, all facing counterclockwise, open position, inside hands joined.

**Timing and Rhythm:** One beat per step (16-beat introduction on FD MH2022).

**PATTERN:**

a. Moving forward (CCW), take 4 walking steps, beginning R. Release inside hands, turn right to face the opposite direction (CW).
b. Rejoin inside hands and moving forward (CW), take 4 walking steps, beginning R, back to place.
c. Release hands, face partner, and step backwards away from partner 4 walking steps, beginning R.
d. Moving toward partner, take 4 walking steps, beginning R.
e. All turn to the right and take 4 walking steps forward (men CW, ladies CCW), beginning R, (away from partner around the circle).
f. Moving backward toward partner, all take 4 walking steps backward, beginning R.
g. Face partner, join right hands (elbow bent), and moving CW around each other, take 4 walking steps, beginning R, once around.
h. Release hands, man moves forward (CCW) with 4 walking steps to a new partner, while lady turns to her right (CW) in place, with 4 walking steps, ready for new partner.

**RHYTHMIC LEARNING CUES:**

|     |                  | R                       |
| --- | ---------------- | ----------------------- |
| a.  | *(To CCW)*       | Forward, 2, 3, turn.    |
| b.  | *(To CW)*        | Forward, 2, 3, face.    |
| c.  | *(Apart)*        | Away, 2, 3, 4.          |
| d.  | *(Together)*     | Together, 2, 3, turn.   |
| e.  | *(To own right)* | Away, 2, 3, 4.          |
| f.  | *(Bwd)*          | Back, 2, 3, face.       |
| g.  | *(Right hands)*  | Turn, 2, 3, 4.          |
| h.  | *(Ptnr change)*  | Change, 2, 3, 4.        |

# APPALACHIAN BIG CIRCLE AMERICAN

This is "square dancing" as the people of the Southern mountains and the Piedmont know it. Descended from British ancestry and father of our Western square dancing, the Appalachian Square dance has an appeal all its own, with its big circle formation and the unique feature of couples visiting around the circle. The "caller" or prompter who leads the dance by calling out the figures is another prominent feature. The traditional figures presented here are a few of the many that are known.

Records:  Capitol T1286; Mercury 20262, or any good square dance record without calls.

**Step:**  A walking step, easy-going and balanced on the balls of the feet, or the step has been described as progressing as if the feet were each in a lid of a shoe box, the dancer being sure to keep his feet low enough not to lose his lids.

**Formation:**  The caller shouts, "Get Your Partner and Form a Ring," at which time couples form a closed single circle. The caller then calls, "Count Off" and starts one couple off with "One!" The man of the next couple (on the right of Number One) shouts "Two," the next man "Three," and so on around the circle to the right (CCW), until all the couples are numbered. One advantage of this dance is that everyone can participate, as long as there is an even number of persons.  Even-numbered couples will remain in place, generally starting the dance figures facing the center of the circle. Each odd-numbered couple starts the figures with their backs to the center of the circle, facing an even-numbered couple.  The odd-numbered couples (called "Ones" or "Odds") complete a figure with the even-numbered couples ("Twos" or "Evens") and then move on around (CCW) the circle to the next Even couple. In this way the Odds progress CCW, visiting each Even couple in turn. The caller often starts and ends the dance with the entire circle performing a figure, or may even break into the middle with some sort of entire-circle pattern.

The caller gives signals for the music to start, "Start the Music," and then calls, "All Left": Dancers join hands around the circle, and all circle to the left (CW) with walking steps. "Halfway Back," says the caller: Hands still joined, all turn and walk back, to place. The caller now might say "Odd couples out and join hands four": All Odd couples move to their right (CCW) and stand with backs to center of circle, facing the Even couple to their right, all hands joined.

**Timing and Rhythm:**  Usually one beat per step on most records.


**SMALL CIRCLE FIGURES:**

> I:    **Circle Left:**  The dancers (Odd couple and Even couple) join hands and circle left (CW).
>
> **The Other Way Back:**  Hands still joined, the 4 turn and circle right (CCW) back about to place.
>
> II:   **Right Hands Cross:**  Release hands, the 2 men join right hands across, the 2 ladies do likewise, while moving around CW.
>
> **Left Hands Back:**  All 4 turn right, the 2 men join left hands, the 2 ladies do likewise, while moving around CCW.
>
> III:  **Bird in the Cage:**  The Odd lady dances into the center, while the other 3 join hands and circle left around her, whistling, making bird noises, etc.
>
> **Bird Hops Out and Crow Hops In:**  Odd man dances into the center, while his partner steps back to rejoin the circle. The 3 join hands and continue circling left around the Odd man, making crow-like noises, etc.
>
> IV:   **Swing Your Opposite, or Swing Your Corner Lady:**  The traditional Appalachian swing is a 2-hand swing, not a buzz-step swing. The hands are joined (man's right with lady's left, man's left with lady's right) about chest high, elbows bent. Partners are a little to the right of each other, bodies almost parallel, and leaning away from each other a little to give balance. In

this position they do a light, easy walking step around each other (CW), about one time around. Your "opposite" or "corner" is the person in the opposite couple of opposite sex. A buzz-step swing is used by many today.

**Swing Your Own:** Release hands with the opposite, turn to your own partner and swing once around.

V:    **Four Leaf Clover:** All 4 join hands around the circle, and **KEEP** all hands joined throughout the figure. Even couple raise their arms (man's right, lady's left) and make an arch. Odd couple ducks beneath the arch, passes thru, then turns halfway around away from each other, while passing their joined hands over their own heads. End with hands crossed (still joined) and all facing each other. Circle left.

**Break That Clover:** Odd couples now form the arch, while Even couples duck and pass through, then form an arch of their own, and pass beneath it, the Even man turning to the left, the Even lady to the right. All 4 will now be back in circle formation, hands joined. Circle left.

VI:    **Lady Around the Lady, and the Gent Also:** The Odd lady, followed by her partner, walks between the Even couple, and the two go behind and around the Even lady, until they are back in place.

**Lady Around the Gent, and the Gent Don't Go:** The Odd lady again walks between the Even couple behind and around the Even man, and back to place, while her partner "don't go"—he stands in his place.

VII:    **Swing Old Adam:** The Odd lady swings with the Even man.

**Swing Old Eve:** The Odd lady swings with the Even lady.

**Swing Old Adam Before You Leave:** The Odd lady again swings with the Even man.

**Swing Your Own.** Original partners swing each other.

VIII:    **Eight-Hands Across:** The 2 ladies join hands while the 2 men join their hands above the ladies' hands.

**Ladies Bow:** The ladies bow, while the men raise their joined hands over the ladies' heads, and behind their backs.

**Gents Know How:** The men duck, while the ladies raise their joined hands over the men's heads behind their backs.

IX:    **Dive and Shoot:** The Odd man, followed by his partner the Odd lady, the Even man, and then the Even lady, (hands kept joined along this line of 4 people) dances through an arch, made by the Even couple and then back to his original position. Without stopping he then continues to dance through an arch made by his partner and the other gent. (The person around whom they dance must turn under his own arm.)

X:    **Gents Stand By While Two Ladies Twirl:** All drop hands, and ladies turn completely around (CCW). Then all rejoin hands.

**Ladies Stand By While Two Gents Twirl:** All drop hands again, and both men turn completely around (CCW). Then all rejoin hands.

**Everybody Twirl:** All drop hands and everyone turns around (CCW). Then again rejoin hands.

XI:    **Wave the Ocean:** Odd couple drops hands of Even couple, dances backward four steps, then forward to face Even couple again.

**Wave the Sea:** Odd couple drops hands, separates and dances around the Even couple executing a do-sa-do behind the Even couple, then dance back to place. (Do-sa-do: passing by the right, and without turning, partners dance around each other back to back.)

**Wave That Pretty Girl Back To Me:**  The Even couple now executes the complete figure.

XII:  **Two Ladies Change:**  All drop hands and the ladies dance straight across the circle, passing by the right, then turn half way round, and all join hands.

**Gents Do The Same:**  All drop hands and the men dance straight through the circle in the same way. All four rejoin hands.

Small circle figures are usually ended with "Swing your Corner. Then your partner. Odd couples move on and circle four."


## BIG CIRCLE FIGURES:

I:  **All Go Left** and **Halfway Back** have been mentioned above. Often-times a caller will follow these with **All Balance In:** The entire circle, hands joined, take 4 walking steps forward toward the center of the circle, often with a great shout. The next call will usually be **Balance Out:** All step backwards 4 steps.

II:  **Promenade:**  All couples walk CCW around the circle, two-by-two, in the promenade position. Usually the man's partner for Promenade is his original partner, other times the nearest lady.

III:  **Grand Right and Left:**  Men face CCW, ladies face CW, all give right hands to the partner and pass him or her by, passing right shoulders. Give left hands to the next and pass that person by, passing left shoulders, and so on moving around the circle, giving alternate hands and passing alternately by right and left shoulders. The caller might call **Half Way Around:** Dancers continue the Grand Right and Left, meeting partner on the opposite side of the room, then usually promenading. Or he might call **All the Way Around:** Continue Grand Right and Left, passing partner once, until meeting partner again about in original place. Or the call might be **Meet Your Partner With an Elbow Swing:** On meeting, partners link right elbows, and go around one time CW making a little circle in place. Advance to the next person, linking left elbows and turning once around. Continue, alternating right and left elbow turns until the next call.

IV:  **Build A Bridge:**  With all couples promenading CCW as in II, the caller might call this figure, building a bridge. One couple, designated as the lead couple by the caller, drops hands, reverses direction, forms an arch (man's left hand and lady's right hand) and dances CW back along the line of advancing couples. Each couple in turn ducks under the arch, then turns to follow the lead couple, making an arch of their own. When the lead couple comes to the end, they reverse direction, assume promenade position, and dance CCW under the arches of the advancing couples. Again each couple in turn follows the lead couple, coming to the end, reversing, taking promenade position, and moving CCW under the arches, until all are again promenading CCW. NOTE: All during this figure the man is on the inside of the circle, the lady remains on the outside.

A typical sequence might go like this:

1. Get Your Partners, Form a Ring.
2. Count Off.
3. Start the Music. All Go Left, Halfway Back.
4. Balance In, Balance Out. Do It Again.
5. Swing Your Partner.
6. Odd Couples Out, and Join Hands Four.
7. Circle Left. The Other Way Back.
8. Right Hands Cross. Left Hands Back.
9. Circle Left. The Other Way Back.
10. Swing Your Opposite. Swing Your Own.
11. Odd Couples Move On.
12. Circle Left. The Other Way Back.
13. Lady Around the Lady, and the Gent Also.
    Lady Around the Gent, and the Gent Don't Go.
14. Circle Left. The Other Way Back.
15. Swing Your Opposite. Swing Your Own.
16. (Other figures are called in any order.)
17. Everybody (the entire group), All Circle Left.
18. Grand Right and Left. Halfway Round.
19. Meet Your Partner, Give Her a Swing.
20. Promenade, Promenade Her Anywhere, Take Her Off to an Easy Chair.

(An imaginative caller will vary his sequence, his pattern as he calls, and the variety of figures, in order to make the dance lively and interesting to all.)

# BELE KAWE

CREOLE-AFRICAN

Pronounced:  BELL-ee KAH-wee

In recent years, folk dancers have "discovered" the excitement of African dances and their derivatives. This dance, apparently from the Caribbean island of Carriacou, was learned from Norma Huff, of Atlanta, Georgia at the 1972 Tennessee Octoberfest Folk Dance Camp.

Record:  AR36, African Heritage Dances.

**Steps:**  Step, touch.

**Formation:**  No partners, free formation. As a rule, most everyone faces in the same direction.

**Timing and Rhythm:**  One beat per step (8 beat introduction on AR36).

**PATTERN:**

PART I:    **Forward Break:** (Men hold the backs of their hands on hip pockets. Ladies, as if holding a long skirt, shaking the ruffles.) Step forward R, both knees bent; step L back in place; step R beside L.

Repeat with opposite footwork (L, R, L).

Repeat Part I three more times (total 4).

PART II:    **Heel Step.** (Arms extended to each side, about shoulder high, bent comfortably.) Touch R heel sideward to right, turning toward the right side, step R beside L.

Repeat with opposite footwork (touch L heel, step L).

Repeat Part II three more times (total 4), moving a little backward the first 2 times and coming forward the last 2 times.

PART III:    **Wheel.** Arms still extended, bend forward at the waist, and move to the right, making a low, wide complete turn (CW) in 3 steps (R, L, R), pause, still bending forward.

Repeat with a CCW turn to the left (L, R, L), pause, still bending forward.

Repeat Part III, one more time (total 2).

**RHYTHMIC LEARNING CUES:**

|  |  | R  L  R  L  R  L |
|---|---|---|
| I: | (*In place*) | Forward, back, close; forward, back, close. |

(*Repeat I, total 4*).

|  |  | R  R  L  L  R  R  L  L |
|---|---|---|
| II: | (*Bwd*) | Heel, step, heel, step, heel, step, heel, step. |
|  | (*Fwd*) | Heel, step, heel, step, heel, step, heel, step. |

|  |  | R  L  R |
|---|---|---|
| III: | (*To right*) | Turn, 2, 3, pause. |
|  | (*To left*) | Turn, 2, 3, pause. |

(*Repeat III, total 2*).

**Styling:** The movement is relaxed, but vigorous and bouncy. In Part III, during the pause, try to shake the shoulders vigorously (almost a vibration), or the men can jump straight up (still bent forward, feet wide apart). At the end, there's music enough for one repeat of Part I (R, L, R; L, R, L) and one Wheel to the right (R, L, R).

When teaching the dance, have the dancers remember 8 Forward Breaks, 8 Heel steps, and 4 Wheels.

**African Drums**

# BOSTON TWO-STEP

ENGLISH

Many ballroom dances of the 1800's are done today as folk dances and have become very popular, especially in England where many clubs specialize in these "old-time" dances. We have here one of the more frequently encountered versions.

**Records:** Folk Dancer MH3001; Folkraft 1158; MacGregor 309; Imperial 1093B and others.

**Steps:** Pas-de-bas, walk, slide, two-steps.

**Formation:** Partners, double circle, all facing counterclockwise, inside hands joined at about shoulder height. Man's left hand is behind his back (as if under a coat-tail), while girl's right hand holds her skirt. Double circle to learn, or free formation. Lady uses opposite footwork.

**Timing and Rhythm:** One pas-de-bas or one two-step per 2 beats (8-beat introduction on FD MH3001).

**PATTERN:**

PART I:    In place and facing forward (CCW), do one pas-de-bas step away from each other (man leaps L, steps R across L, then steps R in place; lady uses opposite footwork), then one pas-de-bas step toward each other.

Moving forward (CCW), take 3 walking steps, release joined hands and turn inward to face the opposite direction (CW).

Rejoin inside hands, and repeat, one pas-de-bas away, one pas-de-bas together, then 3 walking steps forward (CW). End facing each other, both hands joined.

PART II:    Both moving to the man's left (CCW), do one pas-de-bas step.

Both moving to the man's right (CW), do one pas-de-bas step.

Both moving to the man's left (CCW), take 2 sliding steps (step-close, step-close).

Both take closed position, and dance 4 two-steps around CW.

**RHYTHMIC LEARNING CUES:**

*(Man begins L, lady R)*

I:    *(Face CCW)*    Away . . , together . .

Forward, 2, 3, turn.

*(Face CW)*    Away . . , together . .

Forward, 2, 3, face.

II:    To his left, to his right, slide-close, slide-close.

*(Turn)*    Two-step, 2., 3., 4 . .

**AS A MIXER:** Partners turn on 3 two-steps in the last of Part II and then the man moves up to the lady in front of him.

# CRESTED HEN



The dance gets its name from the resemblance of the red stocking cap, worn by the men, to a hen's crest. The girls try to steal the cap from the fellow's head as they go through the arches. If successful, the girl gets a kiss from the fellow.

**Records:** World of Fun M108; Victor EPA 4143.

**Step:** Step-hop.

**Formation:** Trios, preferably one man and two ladies, in free formation, all hands joined.

**Timing and Rhythm:** Two beats per step-hop (the 4-note introduction on M108 takes 8 beats).

**PATTERN:**

PART I:    Moving left (CW), all take 8 step-hops, beginning on L.

Then, do 8 step-hops to the right (CCW).

PART II:    (The two outside dancers release their joined hands and continue to hold the center's hand, to make a straight line of three.)

The right hand dancer with 4 step-hops, goes through an arch formed by the center and right hand dancer, followed by the center dancer who does a right turn under his own right arm.

Then the left hand dancer, with 4 step-hops, goes through an arch formed by the center and left dancer, followed by the center who turns left under his own left arm.

Repeat all of Part II.

**RHYTHMIC LEARNING CUES:**

<pre>
              L         R                    8
I:       Circle-left, step-hop, . . . . . . . step-hop.

              L         R                    8
         Circle-right, step-hop, . . . . . . step-hop.
</pre>

II:    Right, goes, under, then, the, center, turns, around.

Left, goes, under, then, the, center, turns, around.

*(Repeat II)*

Arranged from a description by the Danish Folk Dance Society.

# DOUDLEBSKA POLKA

CZECHOSLOVAKIAN

Pronounced:  Dood-LEHB-ska

A polka mixer which is fun for all ages. This dance was introduced at Michael and Mary Ann Herman's Maine Folk Dance Camp by Jeanette Novak.

Records:  Folk Dancer MH3016; Folkraft 1413; Educ. Dance Record. FD-2.

**Steps:** Polka, walk.

**Formation:** Partners, double circle all facing counterclockwise, promenade or closed position.

**Timing and Rhythm:** Polka, two beats per polka step; walking, one beat per step (8-beat introduction on FD MH3016).

## PATTERN:

PART I:    Moving CCW around the circle, partners do 16 polka steps.

PART II:    Assuming schottische position, with man's free left hand on the left shoulder of the man in front of him, all march forward (CCW) around the circle (men must move sideward to the left to make the circle smaller), all singing loudly Tra-La-La, etc. (This takes 32 walking steps.)

PART III:    (Partners separate, with men forming a single circle facing center.) Men, in polka rhythm, clap own hands twice, clap neighbors' hands once by extending each hand, palm outwards, towards neighbors on each side. Continue this clap pattern (total 16 times).

While the men are clapping, the ladies polka CW around the circle of men.

At the end of Part III, the men turn to the right, and take the closest lady for a new partner and repeat the dance from the beginning.

Those who do not get a partner immediately go to the center of the circle to meet another partner-less person.

Extra people can enter during the clapping part.

## LEARNING CUES:

I:    Polka.

II:    March and sing.

III:    Clap and polka.

*(Clap rhythm: clap, clap, clap, pause.)*

**Styling:** Sprightly and lively. Some groups add fun to Part III. Several of the men swing their ladies into the center of the circle, where they proceed to polka. The ladies may even try to escape from the circle, the men may try (gently!) to prevent their escape. Teaching Hint: Have all the men follow their right hand with their eyes, while handclapping in Part III, so that the clapping becomes smoother and easier.

# GAY GORDONS

An old favorite with many variations, two of which are presented here.

Records:  Beltona 2455; Victor EPA 4129; World of Fun 116; Folkraft 1162.

**Steps:**  Walk, pas-de-bas, two-step.

**Formation:**  Partners, double circle, all facing counterclockwise, inside hands joined.

**Timing and Rhythm:**  One beat per walking step (brief one-note introduction on F 1162).

**PATTERN:**

PART I:   Moving forward (CCW), take 4 walking steps (man begins L, lady R).

Turning in toward partner to face CW, join other hands and take 4 walking steps backward (still moving CCW).

Then dance 4 walking steps forward (CW), (man begins L, lady R).

Turn in toward partner, face CCW, join other hands, take 4 walking steps backward (still moving CW).

PART II:   Balance toward, and then away from partner, doing one two-step or one pas-de-bas step toward, and one away.

With lady passing in front of her partner and making full turn to her left, partners change places with 4 walking steps.

Join new inside hands, and again balance toward, and away from partner.

With 4 walking steps the lady, making a right turn, dances under partner's left arm and to the right side of the man behind, while man dances forward to left side of the lady ahead who becomes his new partner.

**RHYTHMIC LEARNING CUES:**

*(Man begins L, lady R)*

I:   *(To CCW)*   Walk, 2, 3, turn.

"        Back, 2, 3, 4.

*(To CW)*   Walk, 2, 3, turn.

"        Back, 2, 3, 4.

II:   *(In place)*   Balance toward, and away.

Cross, 2, 3, 4.

*(In place)*   Balance toward, and away.

Change, partner, 3, 4.

**TRADITIONAL VERSION:**  In Part II, partners have right hands joined. Lady turns twice around CW with 4 two-steps under joined hands, while man moves forward around circle (CCW) with 4 two-steps. (Cue: lady turns, 3, 4.) Then in closed position, couple turns CW with 4 two-steps while moving CCW around the room. (Cue: couple, turns, 3, 4.)

# GOOD OLD DAYS

AMERICAN

A novelty dance with a Charleston jazz step. Composed by Nina Reeves.

Record: Smash 2010.

**Steps:** Charleston, strut, heel-touch, swivel.

**Formation:** Partners, double circle, all facing counterclockwise, inside hands joined. Can also be done without partners in free formation.

**Timing and Rhythm:** Two beats to "touch heel and step," 2 beats per strutting step (16-beat introduction on S 2010).

## PATTERN:

PART I:    Both touch L heel forward, then bring L back to place and step on it. Touch R heel forward, step R in place. (This is done rapidly.)

With both feet together, flat on floor, quickly swivel or swish both heels apart, then together, apart, and together.

Move forward (CCW) with 4 strutting steps, beginning on L.

Repeat all of Part I.

PART II:    In place, do 2 Charleston steps (step forward on L, point R forward, step back on R, point L backward) with jazzy heel and toe swivels, kicks, etc.

PART III:    Release hands, and turn away from each other (man turns left, lady turns right) making a circle in 8 strutting steps, man moves to the lady who was in back of him for his new partner.

## RHYTHMIC LEARNING CUES:

I:    *(In place)*    L  L  R  R
Heel, place, heel, place, swish, swish.

*(To CCW)*    L
Strut, 2, 3, 4.

*(In place)*    L  L  R  R
Heel, place, heel, place, swish, swish.

*(To CCW)*    L
Strut, 2, 3, 4.

II:    *(In place)*    L  R  R  L
Forward, point, back, point.

L  R  R  L
Forward, point, back, point.

III:    *(Turn)*    Strut, 2, . . . . . . . . . . 7, 8.

# HASAPIKOS



**Pronounced:**  Hah-SAH-pee-kohs

Two major versions exist, a fast Hasapikos, and a slow Hasapikos. The slow version has been called a sailor's dance, and has become quite well-known as Zorba's dance in the movie "Zorba the Greek." The one presented here is the fast version—perhaps also an occupational dance since it is also called the "Butcher's Dance." The origin is ancient, certainly dating back at least to Byzantine times.

**Records:** Folkraft F1021; Parnassus P210; Colonial LP-140; Prestige 13001; and many others.

**Steps:**  Step, step-swing.

**Formation:**  No partners, broken single circle, or line, facing center. Arms in shoulder position.

**Timing and Rhythm:**  One beat per step (8-beat introduction on F1021).

## BASIC PATTERN:

Moving right (CCW), step to the right with R; step on L in front of R; step right with R; swing L in front of R; step on L in place; swing R in front of L. (The swing should be more of a little kick or thrust, rather than a graceful swing of the leg.)

VAR. I:    (Slides)  Sliding steps to the right (as many as the leader decides, usually until the phrase of music ends).

VAR. II:    (Swivels)  Feet more or less together and kept parallel throughout this variation. With weight on the balls of feet, twist both knees to the left, turning the heels to the right and swiveling on the toes. Then transfer the weight to the heels and swiveling on the heels, twist both knees to the right. Continue toe and heel swiveling, moving to the right, usually to the end of the phrase of music.

VAR. III:    (Triplets)  Begin exactly as in the basic step, but instead of doing the step-swings, do 2 triplets.

## RHYTHMIC LEARNING CUES:

```
              R     L     R     L     L     R
Basic:   Right, cross, step, swing, step, swing.
```

Var. I:   Slide, slide, slide, etc.

Var. II:   Swivel, swivel, etc.

```
              R     L     R     L
Var. III:   Right, cross, 1-2-3, 1-2-3.
```

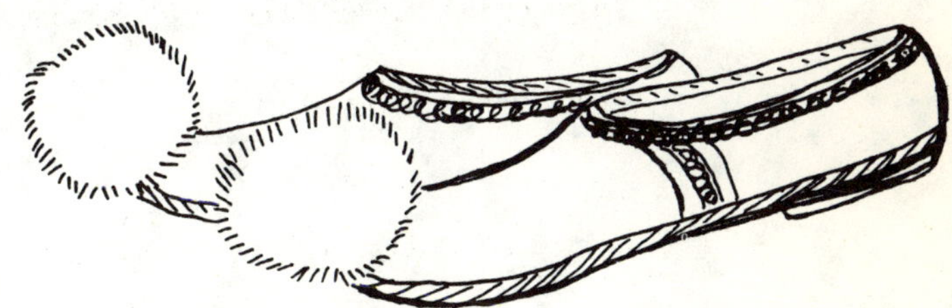

**Styling:**  There are many variations in this dance, only a few of which are described here. The leader is at the right end of the line and changes the step at will. The dancers in the line follow the leader as he maneuvers the line around the dance floor. The movements are lively, vigorous, and forceful.

# HASHUAL Israeli

Pronounced:  Hah-shoo-AHL

Translated "The Fox," this popular dance was composed by Rivka Sturman and learned from Fred Berk, the dean of American teachers of Israeli folk dance.

Records:  Tikva 45-98-2; Tikva T-98-33; Hed Arzi MN529.

**Steps:**  Step, grapevine, two-step, brush.

**Formation:**  No partners, closed single circle, all facing somewhat right, hands joined in basic line position.

**Timing and Rhythm:**  One beat per walk, two beats per two-step (16-beat introduction on Tikva 45-98-2).

**PATTERN:**

PART I:    Moving forward in line of direction (CCW) take seven walking steps, beginning R, clapping hands 3 times while stepping the 3rd and 4th steps. (Hands should be clapped, up in front of the right shoulder, then rejoined.)

Continuing CCW do 1½ grapevine steps (Step L across R, step R to the right, step L behind R, step R to the right, step L across R, step R to the right).

Step L to the left (CW); bring R back to L and then forward again in a U-shaped movement, brushing R against the floor as it is brought near L (R is now free and ready for the next step).

Repeat Part I, ending facing center but with right shoulder leading (pointing somewhat toward center). Release hands.

PART II:    Moving toward the center, bending forward, arms down and snapping fingers on the beat, do 4 two-steps, starting on R.

Step forward on R, bending low and clapping own hands just in front of R knee.

Straighten up, and while bringing arms together forward, then raising high overhead, then circling each sideward and down, take seven walking steps backwards to place, beginning L.

Repeat Part II.

**RHYTHMIC LEARNING CUES:**

<pre>
                          R    L    R   L     R    L    R
    I:      (To CCW)     Step, step, clap - clap - clap, step, step, step.

                          L    R    L    R    L    R
         (To CCW)        Cross, side, behind, side cross, side,

                          L    R
         (In place)      step, brush.

             (Repeat I)


                          R    L    R       L    R    L
    II:     (To center)  Step, close, step, and; step, close, step, and;

                            R    L    R     L    R    L       R
                          step, close, step, and; step, close, step, and; clap.

                          L         L
         (Bwd)           Step, 2, 3, 4, 5, 6, 7.

             (Repeat II)
</pre>

**Styling:** Movement is light and easy. Every second time through Part I, preparatory to Part II, abbreviate the last brush movement — it becomes just a touch (touch R beside L). The forward step R in Part II (after the 4 two-steps) is done with emphasis, almost a little leap forward — it's the climax of the dance along with the hand clap at this point. The two-steps forward are small, so as not to crowd in to the center too much, and the seven steps backward are such as not to spread the circle too much. Some groups have one dancer (the Fox) sit on the floor in the center of the circle during each sequence. This center person grasps the hand of someone of his choice, as they move toward him and clap the second time, thus designating the next one to sit in the middle. For teaching the dance, have the dancers walk through Part I several times without clapping hands, until the footwork is well-assimilated. Then add the clapping.

# HIP HIP POLKA

LITHUANIAN

This is a novelty dance that can be done as a couple dance or as a mixer. In Lithuania it is called "Koja Koja" and means Your Foot, Your Foot. Introduced by Vyts Beliajus.

**Record:** Folkraft 1418.

**Steps:** Two-step, polka.

**Formation:** Partners facing, single circle, men facing counterclockwise, ladies clockwise. Can also be done in free formation.

**Timing and Rhythm:** Two beats per polka step (4-beat introduction on F 1418).

## PATTERN:

PART I:    Each moving to own right, keeping both hands joined take one two-step right (step, close, step, pause), then stamp, stamp (L, R).

Each moving to own left, hands still joined, take one two-step left and a stamp, stamp (R, L).

Again take a two-step to the right. Then "hip, hip" left by bumping left hips twice.

Now take a two-step to the left and "hip, hip" right, bumping right hips.

PART II:    In a closed or shoulder-waist position take 8 polka steps (hop, step, close, step) anywhere in the room.

## RHYTHMIC LEARNING CUES:

```
                        R    L    R         L    R
I:     (To own right)   Step, close, step, and, stamp, stamp.

                        L    R    L         R    L
       (To own left)    Step, close, step, and, stamp, stamp.

                        R    L    R
       (To own right)   Step, close, step, and, hip, hip.

                        L    R    L
       (To own left)    Step, close, step, and, hip, hip.


II:    (Anywhere)       Polka, . . . . . . . . . . . . 7, 8.
```

## AS A MIXER:

PART I:    The same as above.

PART II:    **Version a.**  Men polka CCW in an inside circle while ladies polka CW around the outside. At the end of the 8th polka step take the nearest person for a new partner and repeat from the beginning.

**Version b.**  After Part I, release partner's left hand but holding right hands, begin a Grand Right and Left around the circle doing the 8 polka steps, taking the next person you meet after the 8th step for a new partner. Repeat from the beginning.

# HORA



Jewish settlers in Palestine brought this dance with them from Romania. The Romanian Sarba step which is basic in the Israeli Hora is similar to steps found in other Balkan and Eastern Mediterranean dances. When Israel gained its independence in 1948, the Hora was already so well-known and widespread in the new nation, that it became a sort of national dance. Israelis often dance the Hora for hours, singing and chanting the rhythms when the music gives out.

Records: Folk Dancer MH1052; Folkraft 1110; Educ. Dance Record. FD-2; RCA LPM 1623; Tikva T106; and many others.

**Steps:** Step, step-swing.

**Formation:** No partners, closed single circle, all facing center, arms in shoulder position.

**Timing and Rhythm:** One beat per step (8-beat introduction on F 1110).

**PATTERN:**

BASIC:    Moving left (CW), step L to left,

Step on R in front of L,

Step L to left, swing R in front of L,

Step on R in place, swing L in front of R.

VAR. I:    As the music speeds up, the dancers become inspired, and the steps become livelier and more vigorous:

Step (almost leap) to the left with L,
Step (almost leap) on R across L,
Jump on both feet,
Step (almost leap) on L while swinging R,
Step on R in place, swing L.

VAR. II:    Step (almost leap) to the left with L,
Step (almost leap) on R across L,
Jump on both feet,
Step (almost jump) on L while raising right knee high (keeping R foot close to left leg),
Finish with 3 quick light stamping steps in place (R-L-R).

**RHYTHMIC LEARNING CUES:**

Basic:    *(To left)*    L   R   L   R   R   L
Left, cross, left, swing, right, swing.

Var. I:    *(To left)*    L   R   R   R   L
Left, cross, jump, swing, right, swing.

Var. II:    *(To left)*    L   R
Left, cross, jump, up, R-L-R.

**Styling:** Israelis are proud of their regained independence, and this fierce pride is best expressed in the Hora, in vigorous movements and exuberant freedom.

# HORA MEDURA

ISRAELI

Pronounced: Hora Meh-DOO-rah
A lively hora with a wide range of movements. Choreographed by Yoav Ashriel and introduced by Fred Berk.
Record: Tikva T-106.

**Steps:** Slide, step, grapevine, stamp, run.

**Formation:** No partners, closed single circle, all facing center, hands joined.

**Timing and Rhythm:** Two beats per sliding step, and one beat per walking step (12-beat introduction on T-106).

**PATTERN:**

PART I:    Moving right (CCW), take 4 sliding steps (R-close L, R-close L, R-close L, R-close L).

Moving toward the center of the circle, do 4 walking steps, (R, L, R, L).

Backward to place with 4 walking steps (R, L, R, L).

Repeat all of Part I.

PART II:    Moving left (CW), do one grapevine step (step R across L, step L to the left, step R behind L, step L to the left).

Continuing CW and bending low, do 4 running steps (R, L, R, L).

Continuing CW, do another grapevine step.

In place, stamp R heel forward twice (R, R), raising the arms up high.

Repeat all of Part II.

**RHYTHMIC LEARNING CUES:**

I:    *(To right)*    Slide, slide, slide, slide,

R          R
In, 2, 3, 4; out, 2, 3, 4.

*(Repeat I)*

R    L    R    L
II:    *(To CW)*    Cross, side, behind, side.

R    L    R    L
Down, run, run, run.

R    L    R    L
Cross, side, behind, side.

R          R
Stamp, pause, stamp, pause.

*(Repeat II)*

# IVANICA                                          Yugoslavian

Pronounced:  EE-vah-neet-seh

Although originally a dance for women, as taught by Atanas Kolarovsky all over the United States, this Macedonian dance has become popular with everyone.

Records:  WT-LP-64-701, WT-7001 45 rpm.

**Steps:**  Step.

**Formation:**  No partners, broken single circle or line, all facing somewhat right, hands grasped at shoulder level in barrel position.

**Timing and Rhythm:**  The musical rhythm is slow, quick, quick. The steps either follow the music with a slow, quick, quick; or there are 2 slow steps per musical slow, quick, quick; or there is one slow step and one lift per musical slow, quick, quick. These variations will be indicated below. (Introduction: 8 slow-quick-quick's on WT-LP-64-701.)

## PATTERN:

Moving forward in line of direction (CCW) take six walking steps, R, L, R; L, R, L. (Slow, quick, quick; slow, quick, quick.)

Continuing CCW, take 2 slow steps, R. L. (Music: slow, quick, quick.)

In place and facing center, step R to the right, lifting L leg (Music: slow, quick, quick); step L to the left, lifting R leg (Music: slow, quick, quick); step R to the right, lifting L leg (Music: slow, quick, quick.)

Moving CW backwards, take 2 slow steps, L, R. (Music: slow, quick, quick.)

Step L to the left, lifting R leg. (Music: slow, quick, quick.)

## RHYTHMIC LEARNING CUES:

|            |     |       |     |       |     |      |
|------------|-----|-------|-----|-------|-----|------|
|            | R   | L     | R   | L     | R   | L    |
| (*To CCW*) | Step, quick, quick; step, quick, quick. | | | | | |

|            | R   | L   |
|------------|-----|-----|
|            | Step, step. | |

|             | R   | L   | L   | R   | R   | L   |
|-------------|-----|-----|-----|-----|-----|-----|
| (*In place*) | Step, lift; step, lift; step, lift. | | | | | |

|            | L   | R   |
|------------|-----|-----|
| (*Bwd CW*) | Step, step. | |

|              | L   | R   |
|--------------|-----|-----|
| (*In place*) | Step, lift. | |

**Styling:**  The movement in this dance is very light — the steps on the balls of the feet — light and easy. When raising the legs, men raise their legs so that the knee points toward the center, and the thigh is almost parallel to the floor, foot hanging naturally. Ladies raise the leg just high enough so that the foot barely clears the floor.

# JAVA

AMERICAN

This novelty dance was composed by Constance Mynatt in 1964 and has been popular with students.

Records:  RCA 47-82080 Al Hirt; or any recording of Java.

**Steps:** Strut, jump, step, pivot.

**Formation:** Partners, double circle, all facing counterclockwise, lady to her partner's right, hands joined. Keep inside hands joined throughout the dance. Lady uses opposite footwork.

**Timing and Rhythm:** Two beats per step (16-beat introduction on RCA 47-82080).

## PATTERN:

PART I:    Moving forward (CCW) both take 4 strutting steps (man begins L, lady R).

Do 4 jumps sideward; away from partner (continue to hold inside hands), toward partner, away, together. (The jumps are low, sometimes even resembling galop steps.)

Repeat all of above, on the last jump end facing partner.

PART II:   Man touches L heel diagonally forward and to the left, touches L toe backward, and moving CW, steps on L behind R, steps on R to the right, closes L to R, stepping on L. (Lady uses opposite footwork.)

Repeat moving CCW, (man begins R, lady L).

PART III:  Still holding same hands and facing each other, both take one step sideward CCW (man L, lady R). Then pivot away from each other on this leading foot, continuing CCW, so that partners are back-to-back, then stepping on other foot (man R, lady L). Both then pivot on leading foot to face each other while stepping forward CCW (man L, lady R). Pivot on leading foot, and step CCW once more ending back-to-back.

Release hands and partners turn away from each other, (man to left, lady to right), making a small circle with 4 strutting steps, man moves to the lady who was behind him for a new partner.

The last time through, end with 4 strutting steps forward (CCW), jump away, together, and away. Improvisation here may be fun.

## RHYTHMIC LEARNING CUES:

|  |  | *(Man begins L, lady R)* |
|---|---|---|
| I: | *(To CCW)* | Strut 2, 3, 4. |
|  | *(Jump)* | Away, together, away, together. |
|  | *(To CCW)* | Strut 2, 3, 4. |
|  | *(Jump)* | Away, together, away, face. |
| II: | *(To CW)* | Heel, toe, behind, step, close. |
|  | *(To CCW)* | Heel, toe, behind, step, close. |
| III: | *(To CCW)* | Face, back, face, back. |
|  | *(Turn)* | Strut, 2, 3, 4. |

**AS A COUPLE DANCE:** Use free formation. On the last part of Part III, turn away from partner to make a small circle with 4 strutting steps, ending side-by-side, ready to repeat the dance with partner.

# JUGO

**Pronounced:** YOU-go

Immediately after World War II, when all Europe was disrupted and in chaos, Huig Hoffman, the noted Belgian folk dance specialist, was doing recreational work in the Belgian relocation camps for displaced persons, former slave-laborers of the Nazis. He found a group dancing this dance, but because of the language barriers never knew who they were or from whence they came. He assumed the dance to be of Balkan origin and labeled it "Jugo."

**Record:** Folkraft 337-010 (Romanian Hora).

**Steps:** Walk, point, leap.

**Formation:** No partners, single closed circle, all facing center, hands in front basket hold, right arm over, left arm under.

**Timing and Rhythm:** One beat per walking step (8-beat introduction on F 337-010).

## PATTERN:

PART I:   Moving to the right (CCW), take 3 walking steps R, L, R, and touch L by R, (turning on the touch to face to the left, CW).

Then moving to the left (CW), take 3 walking steps L, R, L, and touch R by L.

Repeat all of Part I three more times (total 4). (End facing center.)

PART II:   Step R sideward to right, pause, close with L, pause.

Point R forward, sideward, and close to L without putting weight on it.

Repeat Part II three more times (total 4).

PART III:   Moving slightly left (CW), leap on R foot leaning forward, leap back on L foot straightening body. Continue leaping forward and back, leaping forward 16 times. (Listen to the music!)

## RHYTHMIC LEARNING CUES:

I:   *(To CCW)*     R    L    R    L
                  Step, step, step, touch.

*(To CW)*     L    R    L    R
                Step, step, step, touch.

*(Repeat I, total 4)*

II:   *(To CCW)*     R    L    R    R    R
                  Step, and, close, and, point, point, close *(no weight)*.

*(Repeat II, total 4)*

III:   *(To CW)*     R    L        16
                Leap, back . . . . . . . . . leap, back.

# KENDİME

TURKISH

Pronounced:  KEN-dee-meh

This simple dance from Western Turkey was introduced by Bora Özkök, of Adana, Turkey, who taught it at the Tennessee Octoberfest Folk Dance Camp in 1973.

Record:  BOZ-OK 101, side 2, band 2.

**Steps:**  Step, touch.

**Formation:**  No partners, broken single circle or line, all facing somewhat right, hands grasped at shoulder level in W formation.

**Timing and Rhythm:**  One beat per step (no introduction on BOZ-OK 101).

**PATTERN:**    (8 counts).

Moving to right (CCW) take 5 walking steps beginning R and turning on last step (R) to face center. Touch L by R, but keep weight on R.

Step L toward center, raise R behind L calf, touching calf with R instep while bending body sharply backward.

**RHYTHMIC LEARNING CUES:**

<pre>
                          R   L R L R   L
        (To right-CCW)    Walk, 2, 3, 4, 5, touch.

                          L   R
   (To center-bend back)  In, raise.
</pre>

**Styling:**  Steps are small and precise, but done in a light, bouncy manner. Keep the arms and hands bouncing up and down continuously, in time with the beat. Both the leader (at the right end of the line) and the left-end person can hold and wave a handkerchief in their free hands. The leader snakes the line up and down around the room so that people often face each other as they pass by.

The Blue Mosque, Istanbul, Turkey

# LILI MARLENE

An arrangement of fundamental folk dance steps to an old tune popular during World Wars I and II.

Records:  Folkraft 1096; MacGregor 310; Old Timer 8070; World of Fun M113.

**Steps:** Walk, slide, two-step.

**Formation:** Partners, double circle, all facing counterclockwise, inside hands joined.

**Timing and Rhythm:** One beat per walking step (8-beat introduction on M113).

## PATTERN:

| | |
|---|---|
| PART I: | Moving forward (CCW), both begin on outside foot (man L, lady R) and take 4 walking steps. Partners face, join both hands, and continuing CCW do 4 sliding steps. Turn individually to face CW, join inside hands, take 4 walking steps forward, (CW). Partners face, join both hands, and continuing CW do 4 sliding steps. |
| PART II: | In place, with both hands joined, both step on L and swing R across, then step on R and swing L across. Repeat the step-swings, L and R. Link right elbows and turn (CW) halfway around with 4 walking steps. Link left elbows and turn (CCW) halfway around with 4 walking steps. |
| PART III: | Both facing CCW with inside hands joined and moving forward (CCW), begin with outside foot (man L, lady R) and take 4 two-steps. Partners turn away from each other (man to left, lady to right) making a small circle in 4 two-steps, man moving to the lady who was behind him for a new partner. |

## RHYTHMIC LEARNING CUES:

I:                      ( *Man begins L, lady R* )

    *(To CCW)*     Walk, 2, 3, 4.
                 Slide, 2, 3, 4.

      *(To CW)*     Walk, 2, 3, 4.
                 Slide, 2, 3, 4.

II:                     ( *Both begin L* )

               L   R   R   L
    *(In place)*    Step-swing, step-swing.

               L   R   R   L
               Step-swing, step-swing.

               CW
    *(Elbows)*     Turn, half, way, around.

               CCW
               Turn, half, way, back.

III:                    ( *Man begins L, lady R* )

    *(Fwd)*      Two-step, 2 . , 3 . , 4 . .

    *(Turn)*     Change, 2 . , 3 . , 4 . .

# MEXICAN MIXER



This is not a truly traditional Mexican dance, but was supposedly introduced into Mexico during the days of Maximilian. Its actual origin is unknown. Popularized by Nelda Lindsay.

**Records:**  RCA LPM1619; Lloyd Shaw 117; RCA EPA4128; "Las Perlitas" from album AFLP 1898 Viva Mexico Vol. 2; or any good Mexican Polka.

**Steps:**  Walk, step-swing, balance.

**Formation:**  Partners, double circle, all facing counterclockwise, promenade position.

**Timing and Rhythm:**  One beat per step (8-beat introduction on RCA LPM1619).

**PATTERN:**

PART I:    Moving forward (CCW), both begin on outside foot (man L, lady R) take 4 walking steps.

Face partners, continue moving CCW as man steps L to left side, steps R behind L, steps L to left side, and swings R over. Lady uses opposite footwork.

Repeat Part I moving CW, reversing footwork.

PART II:    (Form a single circle, men facing the wall, ladies facing center of circle, right hands joined with partner, and left hand to person on your left.) Balance forward and backward (man L, R; lady R, L).

Release left hands and change places with your partner with 4 walking steps.

Join left hands with new person to re-form a single circle with men facing in and ladies facing out. Repeat balance forward and backward.

Release right hands and change places with the lady on your left in 4 walking steps, finishing side by side with her, your new partner.

Repeat dance from beginning with this new partner.

**RHYTHMIC LEARNING CUES:**

I:                              (*Man begins L, lady R throughout*)

(*To CCW*)    Walk, 2, 3, 4.

(*To CCW*)    Step, behind, step, swing.

(*To CW*)    Walk, 2, 3, 4.

(*To CW*)    Step, behind, step, swing.

 

|  |  | fwd     bwd |
|---|---|---|
| II: | (*Single circle*) | Balance, balance. |
|  | (*Right hand*) | Change, 2, 3, 4. |
|  | (*Single circle*) | fwd     bwd<br>Balance, balance. |
|  | (*Left hand*) | Change, 2, 3, 4. |

# NEDA GRIVNE

Pronounced:  NEH-da GREEV-neh

This dance was introduced by the noted Balkan dance authority, Richard Crum. It is a very graceful and calm kolo known to some as "Pretty Neda" and to others as "Neda's Bracelet."

Record:  Folk Dancer MH1015.

**Steps:** Walk, balance.

**Formation:** No partners, closed or broken single circle, hands joined and held forward at shoulder level, in barrel position.

**Timing and Rhythm:** One beat per step (no introduction on FD MH1015).

## PATTERN:

PART I:     Moving to the right (CCW), all take 7 walking steps, beginning on R, closing L to R on the eighth beat, and turning to face center.

PART II:    Beginning with L, take 2 slow walking steps to center.

Then take 3 walking steps backward (L, R, L).

Balance right by stepping R to right side and touching L close to it, without stepping on L.

Balance left by stepping L to left side and touching R.

## RHYTHMIC LEARNING CUES:

I:          *(To CCW)*     R
                           Walk, 2, 3, . . . . . . . . . . . 7, turn.

II:         *(Fwd and back)*   L   R   L   R   L
                               In, slow; back, quick, quick, and.

            *(Balance)*    R   L   L   R
                           Step-touch, step-touch.

Serbian (Jugoslavia)

# OSTENDE

AMERICAN

This dance, done to the tune "Selma Schottische," suggests skaters gliding together on smooth ice. It can be done as a couple dance or a mixer. Arranged from Olga Kulbitsky's description.

Record: Folkraft 1048.

**Steps:** Schottische, glide, step-hop.

**Formation:** Partners, double circle, all facing counterclockwise, in promenade position.

**Timing and Rhythm:** Four beats per schottische step, 2 beats per glide (one-note introduction on F 1048).

**PATTERN:**

PART I:    Beginning with R, both take a schottische step to the right (stepping R to the right, step L in back of R, step to right on R, hop on R and swing L across in front of R).

Then do a schottische to the left.

Starting on R, do 4 gliding steps each diagonally forward as if skating on ice.

PART II:    Facing partner, left hands joined, each move to own right with a schottische step beginning R.

Return with a schottische step to the left, and join right hands.

Turn clockwise with partners with 4 step-hops starting R.

**RHYTHMIC LEARNING CUES:**

I:    *(Face CCW)*      R           L
Schottische to the right, schottische to the left.

        *(Diags)*    R  L  R  L
Skate, skate, skate, skate.

II:    *(Face ptner)*    R            L
Schottische to the right, schottische to the left.

        *(Turn)*    R
Step-hop, 2 . , 3 . , 4 . .

**AS A MIXER:**

PART I:    Same as above.

PART II:    Release hands and each take a *long* schottische step to own right, away from partner and passing new partner. (Cue: *long* schottische right.)

Take a *short* schottische step to the left, ending in front of new partner. (Cue: *short* schottische left.)

Join right hands with new partner and turn with 4 step-hops. (Cue: turn, 2, 3, 4.)

Repeat dance from beginning with new partner.

# PLESKAVAC

**Pronounced:** PLAYSS-kah-vahts

Some folk dance groups frequently start the evening with this dance.

**Records:** Folk Dancer MH1009; Folkraft 1548 × 45.

**Steps:** Step, stamp.

**Formation:** No partners, closed or broken single circle all facing center, hands joined in V-position.

**Timing and Rhythm:** Two beats per walking step, one beat per step or stamp (no introduction on FD MH1009).

**PATTERN:**

PART I:    Moving diagonally forward and to the right, take 2 walking steps (R, L).
In place, do 3 steps (R, L, R).
Moving straight backward from center, take 2 walking steps (L, R).
In place, do 3 steps (L, R, L).

Repeat Part I.

PART II:    Facing center and moving forward directly toward center, take 2 walking steps (R, L).
In place, do 3 stamps (R, L, R).
Moving backward, take 2 walking steps (L, R).
Release hands and clap 3 times.

Repeat Part II.

**RHYTHMIC LEARNING CUES:**

I:      *(To diag)*    Right, and, left, and, step, step, step.
    *(Bwd)*    Left, and, right, and, step, step, step.

Part I

*(Repeat I)*

II:      *(To center)*    Right, and, left, and, stamp, stamp, stamp.
    *(Bwd)*    Left, and, right, and, clap, clap, clap.

*(Repeat II)*

**Styling:** Leader (at right end of the broken line) can change the walking steps into skipping steps at times, to liven things up. Then the circle expands. When the circle closes together the leader might simmer down to walking steps again. The leader can weave the line as he wishes around the room.

Dick Crum, who taught this dance at the East Tennessee Fall Folk Dance, learned it from Jugoslavian musicians playing at the Herman's Folk Dance House in New York City.

# POLSTER TANC



Pronounced:  POHL-stir Tahnts

In Jugoslavia, when the guests did this wedding dance, the male dancer, who had been embraced, left the circle and gave a donation of money to be turned over to the newlyweds. Dick Crum brought this dance to the United States.

Record:  Folk Dancer MH3034.

**Steps:** Waltz, polka.

**Formation:** No partners, closed single circle, hands joined. One person in the center of the circle (preferably starting with a man) holding a pillow in his hands. In our country, we can do the dance without anyone leaving the circle or giving donations.

**Timing and Rhythm:** One beat per step (no introduction on FD MH3034).

**PATTERN:**

PART I:    Moving left (CW), all take 8 waltz steps, while man in center, moving right, looks for a partner; Moving right (CCW), 8 waltz steps; center person moves left, still looking.

PART II:    Center man chooses a lady, places the pillow on the floor in front of her, both kneel and kiss and/or embrace. The circle stops dancing during this interval.

PART III:    The kneeling couple stand up and polka together in the circle, carrying the pillow with them, while the circle dances polka steps, first 8 polka steps moving left, then 8 to the right.

*Repeat from the beginning, the man joining the circle (or leaving), and girl now preparing to make her choice. Continue this alternation.*

**LEARNING CUES:**

I:    All (*except center person*) waltz left, then right. $^8$ $^8$

II:    Couple embraces, while circle stands.

III:    All polka left, then right, while center couple polka. $^8$ $^8$

**Styling:** Both the polka and the waltz are done in a lively, spirited manner, to express the joyousness of the wedding party. The dancers can sing or shout as heard on the record.

# POSKOK

**Pronounced:** POHS-kohk

This lively Serbian dance was learned from Vyts Beliajus at the 1970 East Tennessee State University Octoberfest Folk Dance Camp.

**Record:** Folkraft 1533 x 45B.

**Steps:** Step, hop, schottische.

**Formation:** No partners, broken single circle, or lines, all facing center, hands joined in V-position, leader at the right end of the line.

**Timing and Rhythm:** One beat per step or hop (no introduction on F1533).

## PATTERN:

PART I:    Moving diagonally forward to the right, step on R, hop on R, step on L, hop on L.

Now, moving diagonally backwards to the right, step R backward, step L backward, step R backward, hop on R. This movement forms an inverted-V toward and away from center.

Repeat the diagonal forward to the left, but with opposite footwork (L, hop, R, hop).

Then move backwards diagonally left (L, R, L, hop).

Repeat Part I.

PART II:    All facing and moving right (CCW), do 8 light, running schottische steps beginning R (R, L, R, hop; L, R, L, hop, etc.).

## RHYTHMIC LEARNING CUES:

I.    (*Diag. right*)    R    R    L    L
             Right, hop, left, hop.

      (*Diag. bwd*)    R    L    R    R
             Back, step, step, hop.

      (*Diag. left*)    L    L    R    R
             Left, hop, right, hop.

      (*Diag. bwd*)    L    R    L    L
             Back, step, step, hop.

             (*Repeat I*)

II:    (*To CCW*)    R    L    R    L    R    L    R    L
             Schottische, 2..., 3..., 4..., 5..., 6..., 7..., 8....

**Styling:** As in all Serbian dances, the steps are small and light. But this dance lends itself to somewhat more vigor and drive. In Part I, as the dancers begin the diagonals, the first step can be emphasized a little with the arms swinging forward in unison. In Part II, the schottische step is kept very low to the floor. The hop is quite subtle and the free foot is brought forward, barely clearing the floor. If danced in short lines of 5 or 6 dancers, the leader of each line can take his group and have them weave around the room.

# RAKSI JAAK

ESTONIAN

Pronounced:  RAHK-see Yahk

A polka dance for three persons. Introduced by Michael and Mary Ann Herman.

Records:  Folk Dancer MH3007.

**Steps:** Walk, polka.

**Formation:** Trios, all facing center, inside hands joined.

**Timing and Rhythm:**  One beat per step (3-note introduction on FD MH3007).

## PATTERN:

**CHORUS:**   All take one step to the left with L, bring R to L without stepping on R (L, touch R).
All step right with R, bring L to R without stepping on L (R, touch L).
Repeat (L, touch R, and R, touch L).
All take 3 walking steps forward (L, R, L), and swing R forward, but not too high.
All walk backward to place with 4 steps (R, L, R, L).

**PART I:**   **Arches.** All, being sure to keep hands joined, dance 8 polka steps, the two outside dancers move at the same time, crossing first in front of the middle dancer, and then behind. Keeping the hands joined lightly overhead, the three dancers will be forming arches, the left dancer goes under and over, while the right dancer goes over and under.

**CHORUS:**   **Repeat Chorus.**

**PART II:**   **Forward and Back.** Keeping hands joined, the two outside dancers turn to face middle person, join their free hands to make a triangle, and all dance 4 polka steps (the outsiders dance backwards) toward the center of the room.

Outsiders release their joined hands and all dance 4 polka steps back to place, while outsiders turn (dancer on right turning CCW, left dancer CW) under their hands which are still clasped with middle dancer.

**CHORUS:**   **Repeat Chorus.**

**PART III:**   **Tuck-In.** Keeping hands joined, outsiders "tuck-in" by turning in place (the right-hand person turns left, the left-hand person right) all the way around towards the middle person, so that all are facing center. The outsiders then join their free hands, and all three do 4 polka steps forward toward the center, and 4 polka steps backward.

## RHYTHMIC LEARNING CUES:

**CHORUS:**   *(In place)*
    L  R   R  L   L  R   R  L
Step-touch, step-touch, step-touch, step-touch.

*(To center)*
  L     R
Walk, 2, 3, swing.

*(Bwd)*
  R
Walk, 2, 3, 4.

The Tuck-In

**SEQUENCE:**   Chorus. Arches. Chorus. Forward and Back. Chorus. Tuck-In.

# ST. BERNARD WALTZ Eɴɢʟɪsʜ

This old-time dance is lively and done to catchy tune; it is popular both in England and Scotland.

Records:  Folk Dancer MH3019; Folkraft 1162; Educ. Dance Record. FD-3; London 432; and others.

**Steps:** Waltz, step-draw, walk.

**Formation:** Partners, double circle, with man's back to center of circle, closed position. Double circle to learn, otherwise free formation.

**Timing and Rhythm:** Three beats per waltz step (8-waltz-step introduction on FD MH3019 takes 24 beats).

## PATTERN:

PART I:  Moving to the man's left (CCW), both take 2 step-draws starting with man's L and lady's R.

Man takes one step to his left with L, and stamps twice, as lady does same with opposite footwork.

Moving to man's right, both take two step-draws (**NOT** stepping on the trailing foot on the last **step**).

Man moving backwards (lady forward) takes 2 walking steps L, R. (Lady R, L). Man moving forward (lady backward) takes 2 walking steps L, R, (lady R, L).

End releasing closed position.

PART II:  Holding one hand only (man's left, lady's right) and both moving to man's left (CCW), man takes 2 step-draws while the lady does a right face turn under man's left arm in 6 steps.

PART III:  Taking closed position, turn with 4 waltz steps, moving CCW.

## RHYTHMIC LEARNING CUES:

*(Man's cues; lady opposite footwork)*

I:  *(To left)*  
L  R  L  R  L  R  R  
Step-draw, step-draw, step, stamp, stamp.

*(To right)*  
R  L  R  
Step-draw, step-draw.

*(Bwd)*  
L  R  
Step, step.

*(Fwd)*  
L  R  
Step, step.

II:  *(To left)*  
L  R  L  R  
Step-draw, step-draw (lady, turns, 3, 4, 5, 6).

III:  *(To CCW)*  
CW  
Waltz-turn, 2 . , 3 . , 4 . .

**AS A MIXER:**  In Part III, turn with 3 waltz steps, the man moving forward to a new partner on the 4th waltz step.

# SALTY DOG RAG

AMERICAN

This dance is a good illustration of the "folk process" — a catchy melody which invites variation after variation.

Records:  Decca 27981; Black Mountain 1008.

**Steps:**  This is a good dance for practicing nearly every step you know.

**Formation:**  Partners, double circle, all facing counterclockwise; or a line of any number, with arms around each other's waist; or a column each with hands on waist of person in front.

**Timing and Rhythm:**  One beat each per heel and toe, 2 beats per two-step (4-note introduction on D 27981 takes 4 beats).

### BASIC MOVEMENT PATTERN:

Begin on L foot by placing L heel forward, L toe backward, then run forward 3 steps (L, R, L).

Repeat with R heel forward, and R toe backward, and 3 running steps (R, L, R).

Begin on L and take a two-step diagonally forward to the left and a two-step diagonally to the right (step, close, step, pause).

Starting with L take 4 step-hops forward.

### RHYTHMIC LEARNING CUES FOR BASIC MOVEMENT PATTERN:

```
        L   L   L R L
     Heel, toe, run, 2, 3.

        R   R   R L R
     Heel, toe, run, 2, 3.

        L     R     L
     Step, close, step, pause.

        R     L     R
     Step, close, step, pause.

        L      R L R
     Step-hop, 2, 3, 4.
```

## VARIATIONS:

1.  Take 2 running schottische steps instead of the two-steps.
2.  Take 4 step-swings instead of the step-hops.
3.  The above variations can be done in any formation.
4.  This couple variation begins in promenade position. After the L heel and toe, keeping left hands joined, man swings his partner forward to face him on the 3 running steps. After the R heel and toe, she turns under his left arm back into place on the 3 steps.

5.  A more advanced pattern, which we'll call **VARIATION 5,** is danced with partners, double circle, all facing counterclockwise, promenade position:

**PATTERN—VARIATION 5:**

PART I:    Moving to the right, both step sideward to right on R, step on L behind R, step to right on R, and brush L foot forward.

Moving to the left, repeat this sequence (step sideward on L, step on R behind L, step sideward on L, brush R).

Walk forward with 4 step-brushes (because of the strong up-beat in the music this feels more like brush-steps than step-brushes).

Repeat all of Part I.

PART II:    (Partners facing, left hands joined, men with backs to center of circle.) Each moving to own right, while keeping left hands joined, do the side, behind, side, brush (R, L, R, brush L).

Each moving sidewards to own left, repeat the side, behind, side, brush (L, R, L, brush R), changing to a right hand hold while moving to the left.

Keeping right hands joined, elbows bent, turn CW with 4 strutting steps back to place.

Repeat all of Part II.

**RHYTHMIC LEARNING CUES FOR VARIATION 5:**

I:    *(To right)*    R    L    R    L
                     Step, behind, step, brush.

     *(To left)*    L    R    L    R
                    Step, behind, step, brush.

     *(Fwd)*    R    L    L    R    R    L    L    R
                Step-brush, step-brush, step-brush, step-brush.

     *(Repeat I)*

II:    *(Left hand)*    R    L    R    L
                       Right, behind, step, brush.

      *(Right hand)*    L    R    L    R
                        Left, behind, step, brush.

      *(Right hand)*    R
                        Strut, 2, 3, 4.

      *(Repeat II)*

## A VARIATION ON PART II OF PATTERN NO. 5:

Each move sidewards to own right with a step, behind, step, brush.

Then turn once around to the left with 3 steps (L, R, L, pause). Clap own hands on the pause, then join right hands and turn with 4 strutting steps.

**AS A MIXER:** Another interesting possibility is to make a mixer out of any of the variations of this dance. On the last four steps, the man moves to a new partner.

Mary Ann Herman attributes the basic version of this dance to Frank Hamilton (American Round Dance Handbook. 1957, Sets in Order), and taught it at the East Tennessee State University Fall Folk Dance.

# SAVILA SE BELA LOZA                                    SERBIAN

Pronounced: Sah-VEE-lah Say BEH-lah LOH-zha

This lively dance comes from the district of Sumadija, Serbia, and means, "A grapevine entwined itself."

Record: Folkraft 1496 × 45.

**Steps:** Run, schottische.

**Formation:** No partners, broken single circle or line, facing somewhat right. Short lines are preferred for this dance. Hands joined in V-position.

**Timing and Rhythm:** One beat per running step (no introduction on F 1496).


**PATTERN:**

PART I:    Moving to the right (CCW), take 19 small running steps, starting with R. End with a hop on R for count 20, while turning to face left.

Moving left (CW), take 19 running steps, beginning with L, and ending with a hop on L, for count 20, facing center.

PART II:   Moving sidewards, do 6 schottische steps (step, step, step, hop) moving first to the right, then to the left, then right, left, right, and left.


**RHYTHMIC LEARNING CUES:**

|     |            | R    L                          19   20 |
|-----|------------|-----------------------------------------|
| I:  | *(To CCW)* | Run, run, . . . . . . . . . . . . . run, hop. |
|     | *(To CW)*  | L    R                          19   20 |
|     |            | Run, run, . . . . . . . . . . . . . run, hop. |

| II: | *(Face center)* | Right, 2, 3, hop; left, 2, 3, hop. |
|-----|-----------------|------------------------------------|
|     | "               | Right, 2, 3, hop; left, 2, 3, hop. |
|     | "               | Right, 2, 3, hop; left, 2, 3, hop. |


**Styling:** The schottische steps in Part II are very controlled and small. The hop is light and should not become a kick. The fun of this dance is found in the movement of the many short lines as they maneuver around the dance floor.


Dick Crum discovered this dance, but acknowledges Dennis Boxell as the one who popularized it in our country.

# SELJANČICA


Pronounced:  Sell-YAHN-chee-tsa

This dance is sometimes called "Djacko" or "Student Kolo."

Records:  Folk Dancer MH1006; Jugoton C6259; Educ. Dance Record. FD-2.

**Steps:** Step, touch, run.

**Formation:**  No partners, broken single circle, all facing center, hands joined and down in V-position.

**Timing and Rhythm:**  One beat per step (no introduction on FD-2).

## PATTERN:

PART I: Moving a little right (CCW), step on R sideward to right, close L to R, step on R to right, and bring L heel to R instep without stepping on L (step R, close L, step R, touch L).

 Moving left (CW), repeat with opposite footwork (step L, close R, step L, touch R).

 Repeat Part I.

PART II: Step on R sideward to the right, bring L heel to R instep without stepping on L (step, touch).

 Repeat with opposite footwork (step L, touch R).

 Repeat Part II.

PART III: Moving to the right (CCW) take 7 light running steps, beginning on R, pivoting on the last step to face left (CW).

 Moving left (CW), take 7 running steps, beginning on L, ending facing center.

## RHYTHMIC LEARNING CUES:

        R  L  R  L
I:  *(To CCW)* Step, close, step, touch.

        L  R  L  R
  *(To CW)* Step, close, step, touch.


  *(Repeat I)*


        R  L  L  R
II:  *(In place)* Step, touch, step, touch.


  *(Repeat II)*


        R       L 7
III:  *(To CCW)* Run, . . . . . . . . . . . run, turn.

        L       R 7
  *(To CW)* Run, . . . . . . . . . . . run, run.

**Styling:**  Serbs are a proud people. When they dance, the body is held erect, but not stiff. The steps are small and crisp.

Dick Crum and Mary Ann Herman together popularized this traditional dance originally learned from Jugoslavian immigrants.

# SHIBOLET BASADEH ISRAELI

Pronounced: Shee-BOH-let BAH-sah-DAY

This dance is done in Israel as a revival of an ancient Passover ceremony in which the first sheaves of barley harvested in the fields were brought and presented to the Holy Temple. This version is danced by an entire circle of dancers, but some folk dance groups do an exciting couple version of Shibolet Basadeh that is interesting to watch and not too difficult to learn. Composed by Leah Bergstein.

Records: Folk Dancer MH1150; EKL 206; Folkraft LP-12; Tikva T106.

**Steps:** Slide, step-hop.

**Formation:** No partners, closed single circle, all facing center, hands joined. Another hand version: hands palm-to-palm with neighbors, at shoulder height.

**Timing and Rhythm:** Two beats per slide-close (12-beat introduction on FD MH1150).

**PATTERN:**

PART I:    **Slide steps facing center; slide steps backs to center.**  Moving sideward to the right (CCW), do 3 slide steps starting on R (R-close L, R-close L, R-close L).

Release hands and step-hop on R, turning to the right halfway around with backs to center.

With hands joined again, do 3 slide steps sideward to the left (still moving CCW) starting on L. Release hands, step-hop on L, turning left to face center.

Repeat all of Part I. End facing right (CCW), hands joined, (palm-to-palm dancers also join hands at this point).

PART II:    **Step-hops forward; step-hops backward.**  Moving forward (CCW), take 2 step-hops, starting on R, and turning left on the last step-hop to face CW. Still holding hands, dance 2 step-hops backward (still moving CCW), turning right on the last step-hop to face CCW.

Repeat all of Part II. End facing center, hands joined.

PART III:    **Step-hops in and out.**  Take 2 giant step-hops to the center (R-hop, L-hop) then 4 small step-hops backward (the hop is minimized, R-hop, L-hop, R-hop, L-hop) to open the circle again.

**RHYTHMIC LEARNING CUES:**

I:    *(To right)*    
R   L    R    L    R    L    R   R  
Slide-close, slide-close, slide-close, right-turn.

*(To left)*    
L    R    L    R    L    R    L    L  
Slide-close, slide-close, slide-close, left-turn.

*(Repeat I)*

II:    *(To CCW)*    
R    L    R    L  
Forward, step-hop, backward, step-hop.

*(To CCW)*    
R    L    R    L  
Forward, step-hop, backward, step-hop.

III:    *(To center)*    
R    L  
In-hop, step-hop.

*(Bwd)*    
R    L    R    L  
Step-hop, step-hop, step-hop, step-hop.

# SNOOPY

AMERICAN

Ann Czompo, from whom the dance was learned, often is credited for composing this interesting novelty dance, but she insists that the original composer is unknown. The name obviously is taken from the popular comic strip character.

**Record:** "Draggin' the Line" SR-3001 (33 1/3); Roulette 7103 (45).

**Steps:** Step, touch, kick.

**Formation:** No partners, free formation. For learning, everyone can face the same direction.

**Timing and Rhythms:** Mostly one beat per step. Both Parts I and II have 8 beats, and 9 movements. Part I is counted: 1, 2, 3, 4, 5, 6, 7-and, 8; or slow, slow, slow, slow, slow, slow, quick, quick, slow. Part II is counted: 1 2, 3, 4, 5, 6-and, 7, 8; or slow, slow, slow, slow, slow, quick, quick, slow, slow. (Introduction: 16 beats, or if preferred one can wait 32 beats until the vocal.)

## PATTERN:

PART I:  Touch L sideward to the left, then bring it back and step on L beside R, touch R sideward to the right, then bring it back and step on R beside L, again touch L sideward to the left, then step on L beside R (6 beats).

Kick R foot forward, step back on the ball of R foot, step on L in place (rhythm: quick, quick, slow; 2 beats).

PART II:  Step on R in place, kick L foot forward, step on L across in front of R, step on R somewhat sideward to the right (4 beats).

Step on L back in place, kick R foot forward, step back on the ball of R foot, step on L in place. Step on R in place while pivoting a quarter turn to the right (rhythm: slow, quick, quick, slow, slow; 4 beats).

*Repeat the dance, making a quarter turn (CW) with each repetition, facing a different wall of the room with each quarter turn.*

## RHYTHMIC LEARNING CUES:

```
           L    L    R    R    L    L
I:     Touch, step, touch, step, touch, step.

       R    R    L
       Kick-ball, step.

       R    L    L    R
II:    Step, kick, cross, step.

       L    R    R    L    R
       Step, kick-ball, step, turn.
```

**Styling:** This is jazz dancing, with loose and fluid movements of the body, arms, and legs. The kicks are kept low. In Part I, the dance may have originally included clapping one's own hands as the dancer stepped in place (touch, clap, touch, clap, touch, clap) after touching the feet sideward.

# SOULTANA

GREEK

**Pronounced:** Sool-TAHN-ah

This Greek dance was learned from Ken Spear of Folk Music International at the 1972 Tennessee Octoberfest Folk Dance Camp. Introduced in the United States by Athan Karras. The song tells about the Sultan's wife, the "Soultana."

**Record:** Chorodrama 4509-A.

**Steps:** Step, touch, run, jump, hop.

**Formation:** No partners, broken single circle, or lines, all facing somewhat right, hands joined in the front basket hold (right arm over, left arm under). The leader, at the right end of the line, can lead his group and weave around the room.

**Timing and Rhythm:** The music has 3 parts — 2 slow parts (vocal) and one fast part (instrumental). In the slow parts, the timing calls for one beat per step. In the fast part, the timing calls for 2 beats per two-step, one beat per jump or hop (16 beat introduction on C4509).

## PATTERN:

PART I:  **Slow Music.** Moving to the right (CCW), take 4 walking steps, R, L, R, L. Step on R to the right, touch L toe across and in front of R.

Step on L to the left, touch R toe across and in front of L.

Repeat Part I seven more times (total 8).

The second time through the dance, Part I is done only 4 times.

PART II:  **Fast music.** Continuing CCW, do 2 light running two-steps, R-L-R, L-R-L.

Facing center, jump on both feet, moving slightly toward the center, hop on R, while kicking L foot forward.

Moving slightly backwards (away from center), do one two-step, L-R-L.

Repeat Part II three more times (total 4).

## RHYTHMIC LEARNING CUES:

I:    (*To CCW*)      
R  L R L  R    L    L    R  
Walk, 2, 3, 4, step, touch, step, touch.

II:   (*To CCW*)      
R   L   R   L   R   L  
Right, two-step, left, two-step.

(*To center & back*)      
L    L    R    L  
Jump, kick, back, two - step.

**Sequence:**  I, 8 times; II, 4 times; I, 4 times; II, 4 times.

**Styling:** Like most Greek dances this is a proud dance — carriage is erect and the bearing is one of great dignity and loftiness, particularly in Part I. In Part II, the two-step is flat-styled, the feet close to the floor, but up on the balls of the feet. The jump to the center is fairly heavy.

# SYRTOS



Pronounced: Seer-TOHS

This dance, and its later variant "Kalamatianos," is danced everywhere in Greece, so that it is a sort of national dance. The oft-told story that frequently accompanies this dance tells how the Moslems, during a long and painful seige of the Greek mountain village of Zalongo, killed all the brave warrior men. The women fought on until they could fight no longer, then formed the ancient chain of the Syrtos and, one-by-one, each danced to her death over the cliff. Frequently the dance is accompanied by song, the leader sings the verses, which the dancers repeat. The role of the leader in inspiring and encouraging the line of dancers is a basic part of the dance. His complicated, improvised steps and turns, vigorous leaps and slaps, spins, gymnastic feats and extraordinary tricks, always keeping in time and position, make a wonderful display arousing the dancers to heights of enthusiasm.

Records: Many records exist; Victor 25-8152; Alpha 2801-B; Liberty 84; World of Fun M 119, etc.

**Step:** Step.

**Formation:** No partners, single broken circle, hands joined at shoulder height, all facing slightly to the right. The leader is at the right end of the chain.

**Timing and Rhythm:** The musical beats, one slow beat plus 2 quick beats, equal the steps described in each section below (slow, quick, quick) and take 4 counts (no introduction on M119).

**PATTERN:**

1. Step forward (in the direction of the line) with R (*slow*), step L forward and in back of R (*quick*), step R forward (*quick*).

2. Step L forward crossing in front of R (*slow*), step R forward (*quick*), step L forward across R (*quick*),

3. Step R forward (*slow*), step L forward across R (*quick*), step R in place (*quick*),

4. Step L to the left to change direction (*slow*), step R across to the left and in front of L (*quick*), step L in place (*quick*), turning to face CCW.

**RHYTHMIC LEARNING CUES:**

|  |  |  |
|---|---|---|
| (*To CCW*) | | R   L   R<br>1. Forward, behind, step. |
| " | | L   R   L<br>2. Cross, step, cross. |
| (*In place*) | | R   L   R<br>3. Step, cross, place. |
| " | | L   R   L<br>4. Step, cross, place. |

# TANT' HESSIE
South African

Huig Hoffman introduced this mixer. Translated, the entire name is "Aunt Esther's White Horse."

Record: Folkraft 337-006B.

**Steps:** Strut, walk, buzz-step swing.

**Formation:** Partners, double circle, with partners facing and slightly apart, men with backs to center.

**Timing and Rhythm:** One beat per step (8-beat introduction on F 337-006).

### PATTERN:

PART I:    Move forward toward partner with 4 strutting steps, beginning L, until right shoulders are to-gether and all dancers are forming a single circle.

Then take 4 strutting steps backward to place.

Repeat Part I meeting with left shoulders.

PART II:    Move forward toward partner, passing right shoulders, and walk around partner back-to-back, and backward to place in 8 walking steps (this is called "do-si-do").

Do a do-si-do passing left shoulders in 8 steps.

PART III:    Extend both arms and catch hold of partner's arm just above the elbows. Turn CW doing a buzz-step swing for 16 steps, pivoting on R and pushing with L ending facing partner as at beginning of dance. (This swing can be done in shoulder waist position, or in closed position modified with man's left and lady's right arm in an elbow grip.)

*The dance is then repeated by moving diagonally forward toward the person to your left for your next partner.*

### RHYTHMIC LEARNING CUES:

|     |                    |                          |
|-----|--------------------|--------------------------|
| I:  | *(Right shoulders)* | L<br>Forward, 2, 3, 4.   |
|     |                    | L<br>Back, 2, 3, 4.      |
|     | *(Left shoulders)*  | L<br>Forward, 2, 3, 4.   |
|     |                    | L<br>Back, 2, 3, 4.      |
| II: |                    | Do-si-do right . . . . 7, 8. |
|     |                    | Do-si-do left . . . . . 7, 8. |
| III: | *(Turn CW)*        | Buzz-step swing . . . . . . 15, 16. |

**Styling:** There are various ways of styling this dance. We suggest that the arms be kept straight and at the sides through the first two parts and that you snap your fingers with the music. Partners look flirtatious-ly at each other throughout the dance, and at the beginning of the last part fling the arms out and shout "Hey" before the buzz-step swing. Or, the dancers can sing Tra-la-la in Part II, and Oompah Oompah Oompah-pah in Part III. This dance has also been described as depicting the age-old story—boy meets girl (Part I, big smiles), boy loses girl (Part II, no smiles), boy gets girl (Part III, Hey!).

# TENNESSEE WIG WALK

There are many versions of this novelty dance. This is a mixer version.

Records:  Decca 9-28-846; King 237.

**Steps:** Schottische, walk, point.

**Formation:** Partners facing, single circle, men facing counterclockwise, ladies clockwise. Right hands joined.

**Timing and Rhythm:** One beat per step (16-beat introduction on D 9-28-846).

**PATTERN:**

PART I:    Point L toe to front, then to side, and then each move sidewards to own right by stepping L behind R, then step R to the right, and closing with L, while changing to a left-hand hold.

Holding left hands, point R toe forward, then sideward. Move to own left by stepping R behind L, L to the side, closing with R, while changing back to right hands.

PART II:   With right hands joined (bending elbows to bring you closer to your partner) turn once around (CW) in place as a couple with 3 schottische steps beginning L (step, step, step, hop).

Now with 3 walking steps (R, L, R) progress forward to the next person, men moving CCW, ladies CW.

*Repeat dance with new partner.*

**ANOTHER VERSION:**  In Part II, turn partner completely around with only 2 schottische steps. Then moving forward (man CCW, lady CW), pass the next person in the circle with a third schottische step, passing left shoulders. Progress on to the next person with 3 walking steps and get ready to repeat the dance with this person. Thus you bypass one person in order to get a new partner.

**NOTE:** A brush can be substituted for the hop in the schottische step throughout the dance.

**RHYTHMIC LEARNING CUES:**

I:    *(To own right)*
     L   L   L   R   L
     Point, point, behind, step, step.

    *(To own left)*
     R   R   R   L   R
     Point, point, behind, step, step.

II:   *(Turn)*
     L      R      L
     Turn, 2, 3, hop; turn, 2, 3, hop; turn, 2, 3, hop.

    *(Ptnr change)*
     R
     Forward, 2, 3.

Arranged from a description by the Folk Dance Federation of California, 1948.

# TETON MOUNTAIN STOMP                                    AMERICAN

Adapted by Doc Alumbaugh from an old-time dance. It has become well known among many folk dancers.
Records: Windsor 7615; Western Jubilee 725.

**Steps:** Step, walk, stamp, two-step.

**Formation:** Partners facing, single circle, men facing counterclockwise, ladies clockwise. Two-hand position to learn, otherwise closed position.

**Timing and Rhythm:** One beat per step (8-beat introduction on W 7615).

**PATTERN:**

PART I:    Both move sidewards toward center of the circle with a step, close, step, stamp (starting man L, lady R).

Do the same action away from the center, step, close, step, stamp (starting man R, lady L).

Take one step sideward toward the center (man L, lady R), then stamp the other foot.

Take one step away from center (man R, lady L), and stamp with free foot.

PART II:    (Partners take banjo position, right sides adjacent.)

Moving CCW, man (starting L) walks forward 4 steps as lady (starting R) walks backward 4 steps.

On the fourth step both do a half turn to the right so that left sides are together. (Man is still in the inside circle and lady is in the outside circle.)

Man walks 4 steps backward (starting L), while lady takes 4 steps forward (starting R) both still moving CCW. On the fourth step they do a half turn to the left. Releasing hands each walks forward (man CCW, lady CW) 4 steps, passing right shoulders, to meet a new partner.

PART III:    Using two-hand position or closed position, new partners turn CW with 4 two-steps (in closed position, can use buzz-step swing).

**RHYTHMIC LEARNING CUES:**

I:                                    (*Man begins L, lady R*)

(*To center*)    Step, close, step, stamp.

(*Out*)    Step, close, step, stamp.

   I       O
Step, stamp, step, stamp.

II:        (*To CCW*)    Walk, 2, 3, turn.

(*Still CCW*)    Walk, 2, 3, turn.

(*Man CCW
Lady CW*)    Change, 2, 3, 4.

III:                                    Turn . . . . . . . . . . 7, 8.

# TEXAS SCHOTTISCHE



This dance is called a schottische; however, it is actually a two-step dance. It is a good mixer and can be used for trios as well as couples.

Records: Victor 45-6177; Decca 447-0184; Decca 23759; or any slow schottische.

**Steps:** Walk, two-step, heel-and-toe.

**Formation:** Partners, double circle, all facing counterclockwise, in varsovienne position.

**Timing and Rhythm:** Four beats per two-step, 2 beats per walking step (16-beat introduction on D 23759).

## COUPLE PATTERN:

PART I:    Moving diagonally forward to the left, both take one two-step, beginning on L (step, close, step, pause).

Move diagonally forward to the right with a two-step.

PART II:    Move forward (CCW), with 4 walking steps, beginning L.

PART III:    Both do a heel-and-toe with L, release right hands and the lady walks across in front of partner with 3 walking steps, turning around to face CW, while man steps in place.

Both do a heel-and-toe with R, still holding left hands, (man facing CCW and lady facing CW), release left hands, and the lady beginning R takes 3 steps CW to man in back of her partner, ending in the varsovienne position, ready to repeat the dance.

## RHYTHMIC LEARNING CUES:

I:    *(Diag left)*
      L   R   L
      Step, close, step, and.

    *(Diag right)*
      R   L   R
      Step, close, step, and.

II:    *(To CCW)*
      L
      Walk, 2, 3, 4.

III:    *(Lady cross)*
      L      L      L  R  L
      Heel, and, toe, and, halfway, round.

    *(Lady back)*
      R      R      R  L  R
      Heel, and, toe, and, move, on, back.

**TRIO PATTERN:**

The groups of three people stand side by side, around the circle, all facing CCW. Outside dancers join inside hands behind center dancer's back, while the center holds their outside hands.

PARTS I and II: Same as Parts I and II of couple pattern.

PART III:    All three do a heel-and-toe with L.

The outsiders drop hands in back of center, (while still holding center's hands) and take 3 steps beginning L to move forward and turn to face the center dancer. Center meanwhile takes his 3 steps in place. (In this position, the center dancer is still facing CCW, while the outsiders are facing CW.)

Now, all do a heel-and-toe with R. Release hands and center takes 3 steps (beginning R) to move forward to become the center dancer of the trio ahead, while the outsiders take 3 steps in place waiting for the center from the trio behind to step up and re-form their trio.

**RHYTHMIC LEARNING CUES:**

I:        (*Diag. left*)    
L R L  
Step, close, step, and.

         (*Diag. right*)    
R L R  
Step, close, step, and.

II:       (*To CCW*)    
L  
Walk, 2, 3, 4.

III:      (*Outs turn*)    
L L L R L  
Heel, and, toe, and, halfway, round.

         (*Center Fwd*)    
R R R L R  
Heel, and, toe, and, move, on, through.

Mary Ann Herman learned this version from Jane Farwell, and taught it at the East Tennessee State University Fall Folk Dance.

**American**

# TROIKA

Pronounced: TROY-ka

This spirited dance suggests "three horses" pulling a sleigh or carriage. Source: Michael and Mary Ann Herman.

Records: Folk Dancer MH1059; Folkraft 1170; Educ. Dance Record. FD-2; World of Fun M105.

**Steps:** Run, stamp.

**Formation:** Groups of three, standing side by side, all facing counterclockwise, holding inside hands. Groups may be three men, three ladies, or preferably composed of both.

**Timing and Rhythm:** One beat per running step (8-beat introduction on FD MH1059).

## PATTERN:

PART I:  Moving diagonally forward to the right, take 4 running steps starting with R.

Next moving diagonally forward to the left, take 4 running steps.

Then moving straight forward (CCW), take 8 running steps.

PART II:  Keeping inside hands joined, and dancing in place with 8 running steps, the person on the right goes through an arch formed by the center person and the left hand person, followed by the center dancer who does a left turn under his own left arm.

The left hand dancer, with 8 running steps, now goes through an arch formed by the center and the right hand dancer, followed by the center dancer who does a right turn under his own right arm.

PART III:  Each trio joins hands in a circle of three and runs 12 steps to the left (CW) and stamps 3 times (L, R, L). Then run to the right (CCW) with 12 running steps ending with 3 stamps (R, L, R).

## RHYTHMIC LEARNING CUES:

I:    (Diag right)    R
Run, 2, 3, 4.

(Diag left)    R
Run, 2, 3, 4.

(Forward)    R
Run, . . . . . . 7, 8.

II:    (In place)    Right, goes, under, while, center, turns, a, round.

"    Left, goes, under, while, center, turns, a, round.

III:    (CW)    L    R    L
Circle, left, . . . . . . . . 11, 12, stamp, stamp, stamp.

(CCW)    R    L    R
Circle, right, . . . . . . . 11, 12, stamp, stamp, stamp.

**AS A MIXER:** This dance may be done as a mixer by having the center person move forward to the next set while the other two dancers do the last three stamps.

# TWELFTH STREET RAG

AMERICAN

A novelty dance with a Charleston beat. Learned at the Maine Folk Dance Camp.

Records: Capitol 1638; MacGregor 748.

**Steps:** Strut, Charleston, point, step.

**Formation:** Couples or groups (up to 4-5) arranged in lines around the room like the spokes of a wheel, all facing counterclockwise, to learn. Or, free formation.

**Timing and Rhythm:** Two beats per strutting step (16-beat introduction on C 1638).

**PATTERN:**

PART I:  Moving forward, take 4 strutting steps (L, R, L, R).

Point L toe forward, point L toe to left side, take 3 quick steps in place, or moving to the right (L, R, L).

Again moving forward, take 4 strutting steps (R, L, R, L).

Then point R toe forward, then to the right side, finish with 3 quick steps in place, or to left (R, L, R).

PART II:  Moving to the left (toward center of circle), do 7 quick steps (L, R, L, R, L, R, L).

Then 7 quick steps to the right back to place (R, L, R, L, R, L, R). (Free improvisation is in order here—grapevine steps, little shuffle steps, swivel steps, etc.)

PART III:  In place, take 2 Charleston steps (step forward on L, point R forward, step back on R, point L backward) with jazzy heel and toe swivels, kicks, etc.

BREAK:  After every second repeat, there is an interlude or phrase in the music during which:

Jump forward and raise both hands high. Jump backward and bend the knees and either slap both knees or throw hands up in back.

Then turn in place (either direction) taking 4 strutting steps (L, R, L, R). On the 4th step clap own hands or a partner's if two are coupled up. (Again improvisation is very much in order in the break).

**RHYTHMIC LEARNING CUES:**

I:  (*Fwd*)
L
Strut, 2, 3, 4.

L  L  L
Point, point, step, 2, 3.

R
Strut, 2, 3, 4.

R  R  R
Point, point, step, 2, 3.

II:  (*To left*)
L
Step, 2, 3, 4, 5, 6, 7.

(*To right*)
R
Step, 2, 3, 4, 5, 6, 7.

III:  (*In place*)
L  R  R  L
Forward, point, back, point.

L  R  R  L
Forward, point, back, point.

Break:  Jump forward, jump backward.

L
Turn, 2, 3, clap.

# TZADIK KATAMAR



Pronounced: Tsah-DEEK Kaht-a-MAR

Translated "Righteousness shall flourish," and composed by Jonathan Gabait, this dance, learned from Fred Berk, has become popular among folk dancers coast-to-coast.

Record: Hadarim LP-3; Tikva 148.

**Steps:** Step, grapevine.

**Formation:** No partners, closed or broken single circle, all facing somewhat right, hands joined in W-position.

**Timing and Rhythm:** One beat per walk (8 beat introduction on Hadarim LP-3).

**PATTERN:**

PART I:     Moving in line of direction, (CCW) take four steps, R, L, R, L.

Facing center, step R to the right, and with feet fairly wide apart, sway in place to the right, left, right, and left.

Repeat Part I.

PART II:     Moving sideward to the right (CCW), do one grapevine step (step R to side, step L across R, step R to side, step L behind R).

Releasing hands make a complete turn CW, in three steps R, L, R, then step L across R.

Step back on R in place, moving CW step L to the left, and step R across L (facing CW), step L back in place.

Step to the right on R with feet fairly wide apart and facing center, in place sway right, left, right, left.

Repeat Part II.

**RHYTHMIC LEARNING CUES:**

I:     (*To CCW*)     R   L   R   L
Step, step, step, step.

(*In place*)     R   L   R   L
Sway, sway, sway, sway.

(*Repeat I*)

II:     (*Swd-CCW*)     R   L   R   L
Side, cross, side, behind.

R   L R   L
Turn, 2, 3, cross.

R   L   R   L
Back, side, cross, back.

(*In place*)     R   L   R   L
Sway, sway, sway, sway.

(*Repeat II*)

**Styling:** The dance is done with bouncy elasticity and verve.

# V'DAVID

ISRAELI

Pronounced:  VAY Dah-VEED

A fast-moving mixer, similar to the American dance "Oh Susannah," and the English dance "Circassian Circle."

Records:  Folk Dancer MH1155; Folkraft 1432; Tikva T-106.

**Steps:** Walk, buzz-step swing.

**Formation** Partners, double circle, all facing counterclockwise, inside hands joined.

**Timing and Rhythm:** One beat per step (16-beat introduction on FD MH1155).

## PATTERN:

PART I:      Moving forward (CCW), take 4 walking steps (man begins L, lady R).

In 4 walking steps, men back up while turning to face the center while ladies step more or less in place, so that all are facing the center of the circle. Then all join hands to make a single circle.

Moving towards center of the circle, all take 4 walking steps forward, then 4 steps backward to place.

PART II:    Releasing hands, ladies take 4 walking steps forward toward center of the circle, then 4 steps backward, while men clap hands.

Men now take 4 walking steps forward toward the center of the circle, turn halfway around to the right, and take 4 steps forward towards the ladies—not to their original partner, but to the lady who is on the right of original partner.

Both now place right arms around partner's waist, and in Hungarian-turn position (see p. 13) do an 8-count buzz-step swing.

*Repeat from the beginning with new partner, man being sure to place new lady on his right after the swing.*

## RHYTHMIC LEARNING CUES:

I:                   *(Man begins L, lady R)*

        *(To CCW)*    Walk, 2, 3, 4; join, hands, 3, 4.

      *(Face center)*   In, 2, 3, 4; back, 2, 3, 4.

II:    *(Face center)*   Ladies, in, 3, 4; ladies, back, 3, 4.

                "       Men, in, 3, 4; turn, to, new, girl.

                        Swing . . . . . . . . . . . . . . . . 7, 8.

Composed by Rivka Sturman, introduced by Fred Berk.

# WOODEN SHOES



This is very similar to the favorite dance of the Lithuanians called "Klumpakojis," and is found in similar patterns among the Swedes, Czechs, Italians, and others. Introduced in this country by Vyts Beliajus.

**Records:** Folkraft 1419; Imperial 1007A.

**Steps:** Walk, stamp, polka.

**Formation:** Partners double circle, all facing counterclockwise, inside hands joined at shoulder height, outside hands on hips.

**Timing and Rhythm:** One beat per step (4-beat introduction on I 1007).

**PATTERN:**

PART I:     Moving forward (CCW), take 8 walking steps, (man begins L, lady R).

Release hands, turn inward toward partner, join other hands, and take 8 walking steps (CW) back to place.

PART II:     Facing partner, join right hands about shoulder height, and take 8 walking steps around each other in place.

Reversing, join L hands and take 8 walking steps back around each other. (End facing each other, man's back to center of circle.)

PART III:     With hands on hips, pause for 4 counts, then stamp R, L, R.

Pause again for 4 counts, and clap own hands 3 times.

Place right elbow in palm of left hand and shake right forefinger at partner 3 times. Repeat with opposite hand and elbow.

Then the lady swings her right hand and arm as if to hit her partner, while making a full pivot turn on L to her left, as partner drops to a squat (or ducks).

Repeat all of Part III, except that man swings as if to hit his partner and pivots, while the lady ducks.

PART IV:     Polka forward (CCW) around the circle with inside hands joined, or varsouvienne position, or closed position, 16 polka steps.

**RHYTHMIC LEARNING CUES:**

*(Man begins L, lady R)*

|   |   |   |
|---|---|---|
| I: | *(To CCW)* | Walk, . . . . . . . 6, 7, turn. |
|   | *(To CW)* | Walk, . . . . . . . 6, 7, face. |

|   |   |   |
|---|---|---|
| II: | *(Turn)* | Right, hands, around, . . . . 7, turn. |
|   | *(Turn)* | Left, hands, around, . . . . . 7, face. |

|   |   |   |
|---|---|---|
| III: | *(In place)* | Listen to the music, stamp, stamp, stamp. |
|   | " | Listen to the music, clap, clap, clap. |
|   | " | Right, finger, shake. |
|   | " | Left, finger, shake. |
|   | " | Lady swings and the man ducks fast. |

*(Repeat III, man swinging, lady ducking.)*

|   |   |   |
|---|---|---|
| IV: | *(To CCW)* | Polka . . . . . . . . . . 16. |

**AS A MIXER:**   The man ends the polka of Part IV with his partner, and advances (CCW) to the next lady on the first 8 walking steps of Part I.

Lithuanian

# ZAJEČARKA

SERBIAN

Pronounced:  Zah-yeh-CHAR-ka

Jugoslavian musicians, playing at Michael and Mary Ann Herman's Folk Dance House, introduced this lively dance.

Record:  Folk Dancer MH1003.

**Steps:** Step, threes, step-touch, run.

**Formation:** No partners, open circle, all facing somewhat right, hands joined low in V-position.

**Timing and Rhythm:** One beat per running step (no introduction on FD MH1003).

## PATTERN:

PART I:     Moving right (CCW), take 2 running steps (R, L).

Then do 3 "threes" (3 quick steps in place) first to the right, then to the left, then to the right.

Repeat Part I moving to the left, and using opposite footwork.

PART II:     (Hold joined hands up to head level.)

Moving to the right, step R, step L, step R, touch L by R foot.

Step L to the left, touch R by L foot, step R to the right, touch L by R foot.

Moving to the left, step L, step R, step L, touch R by L foot.

Step R to right, touch L by R foot, step L to the left, touch R by L foot.

## RHYTHMIC LEARNING CUES:

I:     *(To CCW)*
       R   L   R    L     R
       Run, run, 1-2-3, 1-2-3, 1-2-3.

*(To CW)*
       L   R   L    R     L
       Run, run, 1-2-3, 1-2-3, 1-2-3.

II:     *(To CCW)*
       R    L   R    L
       Step, step, step, touch,

       L    R   R    L
       Step, touch, step, touch.

*(To CW)*
       L    R   L    R
       Step, step, step, touch,

       R   L   L    R
       Step, touch, step, touch.

**Styling:** As in practically all Serbian dances, the body is held erect and the steps are small and crisp.

# ZIGEUNERPOLKA

GERMAN

Pronounced:  Tsee-GOY-nehr-polka

A nice mixer in polka rhythm.

Record:  Folkraft LP-5.

**Steps:**  Polka, walk.

**Formation:**  Partners, double circle, all facing counterclockwise, inside hands joined to learn. Later, partners facing in closed position.

**Timing and Rhythm:**  Two beats per polka, one beat per walking step (8-beat introduction on Folkraft LP-5).

### PATTERN:

PART I:    **Polka.** Moving forward (CCW) around the circle, all do 8 polka steps. End facing partner, men's backs to center.

PART II:    **Bowing.** Bow and curtsy to partner.

Bow and curtsy to your left, to the person on the right of your partner.

Bow and curtsy to your right, to the person on the left of your partner.

Bow and curtsy again to partner.

PART III:    **Clapping.** Men moving CCW, ladies CW around the circle, each takes 2 walking steps, clapping own hands together on the first step, then clapping both hands with the person you meet and pass. Continue around the circle, walking and clapping, a total of 8 times, taking the 8th person for your new partner, and repeat the entire dance.

### RHYTHMIC LEARNING CUES:

*(Man begins L, lady R)*

I:    **Polka.**    Polka . . . . . . . . . . . $\overset{8}{\text{polka}}$.

II:    **Bowing.**    Partner.

To your left.

To your right.

Partner.

III:    **Clapping.**    Own, One, Own, Two . . . . . . Own, Eight.

Mary Ann Herman learned this dance from Jane Farwell of Wisconsin and Mount Horeb Christmas Folklore Institute, and taught it at the East Tennessee State University Fall Folk Dance.

# Chapter 7

## *Dance Patterns*
## *Moderately Easy to Learn*

This chapter includes thirty-three moderately easy-to-learn dances. They are arranged alphabetically in groups according to the number of dancers involved in the dances — Non-Partner, Couple, More than Three. Some of the dances can be placed in all three categories. The dances are based on a variety of basic steps.

# ALI PAŞA TURKISH

Pronounced:  AH-lee Pa-SHAH

Turkish folk dances have become very popular among American folk dancers in recent years. This dance from western Turkey is an arrangement of authentic steps by Bora Özkök of Adana, Turkey, as taught at the Tennessee Octoberfest Folk Dance Camp in 1973.

Record:  BOZ-OK 102 Side 1, band 1.

**Steps:**  Step, point, brush.

**Formation:**  No partners, broken single circle or line, all facing somewhat right, hands grasped at shoulder level in W-position.

**Timing and Rhythm:**  One beat per step, stepped off quick, quick, quick, slow. (No introduction on BOZ-OK-102, or wait 32 beats and start on vocal.)

**PATTERN:**

PART I:    **Forward and Back.**  Moving forward in line of direction (CCW) take 3 quick walking steps (R, L, R), point L toe forward (slow).

Similarly, moving backwards (CW) take 3 quick walking steps and touch R beside L (slow).

Repeat, moving forward to center and back from the center.

Repeat all of Part I moving first CCW and backwards, then to center and back.

PART II:    **Grapevine.**  All facing center, move sideward to the right (CCW), step R to the right (quick), step L behind R (quick), step R to the right (quick), step L in front of R (slow). Step R to the right (quick), step L behind R (quick), step R to the right (quick), touch L beside R (slow).

Repeat, moving to the left (CW) with opposite footwork.

Repeat all of Part II, moving sideward to the right and then to the left.

PART III:    **Brush.**  All still facing center, with weight on L, cross R in front of L and brush it backward just to left of L (quick), brush R forward (quick), step R to the right (quick), close L to R (slow).

Repeat the brush, brush, step, close.

Step forward into center on R (quick), step back in place on L (quick), step R beside L (quick), extend L heel forward touching floor (slow).

Step backward on L (quick), step R back beside L (quick), step forward to place on L (quick), lightly stamp R (no weight) beside L (slow).

Repeat all of Part III.

**RHYTHMIC LEARNING CUES:**

|  |  | R     L     R     L |
|---|---|---|
| I: | (*To CCW*) | Step, quick, quick, point. |
|  | (*Bwd CW*) | L     R     L     R<br>Step, quick, quick, touch. |
|  | (*To center*) | R     L     R     L<br>Step, quick, quick, point. |
|  | (*Bwd to place*) | L     R     L     R<br>Step, quick, quick, touch. |
|  | (*Repeat I*) |  |
| II: | (*Swd CCW*) | R   L   R   L   R   L   R   L<br>Side, behind, side, cross. Side, behind, side, touch. |
|  | (*Swd CW*) | L   R   L   R   L   R   L   R<br>Side, behind, side, cross. Side, behind, side, touch. |
|  | (*Repeat II*) |  |
| III: | (*Swd CCW*) | R   R   R   L   R   R   R   L<br>Brush, brush, step, close. Brush, brush, step, close. |
|  | (*Fwd & Bwd*) | R   L   R   L<br>In, back, close, heel. |
|  | (*Bwd & Fwd*) | L   R   L   R<br>Back, close, forward, stamp. |
|  | (*Repeat III*) |  |

**Styling:** Steps are small and precise, but done with a lot of spirit and vigor. Keep the arms and hands bouncing up and down in the basic rhythm of quick, quick, quick, slow. Both the leader (at the right end of the line) and the left-end person can hold and wave a handkerchief in their free hands. In Part I, when pointing the L toe forward (remember that to point means to touch the floor with the toe) the body leans backward a bit. Similarly, in Part III, when touching L heel forward, lean backward a little.

# ALUNELUL ROMANIAN

Pronounced:  Ah-loo-NAY-loo

Introduced by Larisa Lucaci at Mary Ann and Michael Herman's Folk Dance House in New York City. The title means "little hazelnuts." Often called "5's, 3's, and 1's" because the pattern is basically 5 steps, then 3, then one step.

Records:  Folk Dancer MH1120; Elektra EKL-206.

**Steps:** Step, stamp.

**Formation:** No partners, closed or broken single open circle, all facing center, arms in shoulder position.

**Timing and Rhythm:** One beat per step (12-beat introduction on FD MH1120).

**PATTERN:**

PART I:    **Fives.**  Moving to the right (CCW), step sideward to right on R.
Step on L behind R. Step again to right on R.
Step on L behind R. Step again to right on R.
Stamp with L heel twice near R. Pause.
Repeat Part I moving sideward to left (CW), but reversing footwork.
Do Part I again to the right, and once more to the left.

PART II:    **Threes.**  Moving right, step on R sideward to the right.
Step on L behind R. Step to right on R.
Stamp L heel near R.
Repeat Part II moving sideward to the left, reversing footwork.
Do Part II again to the right, and once more to the left.

PART III:    **Ones.**  Step R in place. Stamp L heel near R.
Step L in place. Stamp R heel near L.
Step R in place. Stamp L heel twice near R.  Pause.
Repeat Part III, reversing footwork.

**RHYTHMIC LEARNING CUES:**

I:     *(To CCW)*     R    L    R    L    R    L    L
                      Step, behind, step, behind, step, stamp, stamp.

       *(To CW)*      L    R    L    R    L    R    R
                      Step, behind, step, behind, step, stamp, stamp.

            *(Repeat I)*

II:    *(To CCW)*     R    L    R    L
                      Step, behind, step, stamp.

       *(To CW)*      L    R    L    R
                      Step, behind, step, stamp.

            *(Repeat II)*

III:   *(In place)*   R    L    L    R    R    L    L
                      Step, stamp, step, stamp, step, stamp, stamp.

       *(In place)*   L    R    R    L    L    R    R
                      Step, stamp, step, stamp, step, stamp, stamp.

# AMERICAN SCHOTTISCHE



There are many variations of this dance which are based upon similar combinations of schottische steps and step-hops. This one should be danced in a vigorous, spirited fashion. As learned from Helen Watson.

**Records:** Capital 4018; Imperial 45-6046; or any good schottische record.

**Steps:** Scottische, step-hop.

**Formation:** Partners, double circle, all facing counterclockwise, inside hands joined, outside hands on hips.

**Timing and Rhythm:** One beat per step (8-beat introduction on Imp. 45-6046).

## PATTERN:

PART I:    **Right Hand Turn.** Moving forward (CCW) take 2 running schottische steps (run, run, run, hop), (man begins L, lady R).

Join right hands (keeping right arm straight). Make a clockwise turn while continuing to progress CCW around the circle with 4 step-hops (man begins L, lady R).

PART II:    **Left Hand Turn.** Moving forward (CCW) do 2 more running schottische steps. Join left hands and make a CCW turn, with 4 step-hops, still progressing CCW around the circle.

PART III:    **Circles.** Still moving CCW do 2 more running schottische steps. Then place both hands on own hips, and beginning on outside foot turn away from partner with 4 step-hops each making a small circle (men turn CCW, ladies CW) ending with partners side-by-side.

PART IV:    **Diamond.** With hands still on hips, take one running schottische step, partners separating with man moving diagonally forward left toward center of circle and lady moving diagonally forward right.

Man now moves diagonally forward to his right while lady moves diagonally forward to her left with one running schottische step, to come together face-to-face.

In shoulder-waist position, couples make a clockwise turn with 4 step-hops (man begins L, lady R).

## RHYTHMIC LEARNING CUES:

*(Man begins L, lady R)*               **Floor Pattern**

I:    **Right Hand Turn.**    Run, 2, 3, hop; run, 2, 3, hop.

Right-hands, step-hop, step-hop, step-hop.

Right hand

II:    **Left Hand Turn.**    Run, 2, 3, hop; run, 2, 3, hop.

Left-hands, step-hop, step-hop, step-hop.

Left hand

III:    **Circles.**    Run, 2, 3, hop; run, 2, 3, hop.

Small-circle, step-hop, step-hop, step-hop.

Each circles

Diamond

IV:    **Diamond.**    Out, 2, 3, hop; in, 2, 3, hop.

Both turn, step-hop, step-hop, step-hop.

Together turn

# BLACK HAWK WALTZ AMERICAN

An "Old-time" dance in waltz rhythm.

Records: Folk Dancer MH3022; Folkraft 1046; MacGregor 309; Imperial 1006.

**Steps:** Waltz, step, point.

**Formation:** Partners, facing, single circle, men facing counterclockwise, ladies clockwise. Two-hand position to learn—later, closed position, free formation.

**Timing and Rhythm:** One beat per step (12-beat introduction on FD MH3022).

## PATTERN:

PART I:    **Balance and Waltz.** Man steps forward on L (count 1, 2, 3), then steps backward on R (count 1, 2, 3), while lady steps backward on R, then forward on L.

Both moving CCW, now take 2 waltz steps, man starting L and moving forward, lady on R and moving backwards. (In closed position, partners can do 2 waltz turns.)

Repeat all of Part I three more times (total 4).

PART II:    **The Crossover.** Man crosses L over in front of R and steps on L (count 1, 2, 3).

Step R over and across L (count 1, 2, 3). Step L over and across R (count 1); step R sidewards to the right (count 2); step on L behind R (count 3).

Point R to right side and hold for 3 counts.

Man repeats the above by beginning with R and crossing it over L and stepping on R (count 1, 2, 3).

Step L over and across R (count 1, 2, 3). Step R over and across L (count 1); step L to left side (count 2); step on R behind L (count 3).

Point L to left side and hold for 3 counts.

(Lady does exactly the same except she begins the Crossover first with R and then with L.)

Repeat all of Part II.

## RHYTHMIC LEARNING CUES:

I:    **Balance, Waltz.**    (*Man begins L, lady* R)

(*To CCW*)    Balance . , balance . , waltz . , waltz . .

(*Repeat I—total 4*)

II:    **Crossover.**    (*Man begins L, lady* R)

(*In place*)    Cross . , cross . .

(*To wall*)    Cross, step, step, point . .

(*Man begins R, lady* L)

(*In place*)    Cross . , cross . .

(*To center*)    Cross, step, step, point . .

(*Repeat II*)

# BLACK NAG

ENGLISH

This is one of the most popular English country dances. The English had a custom of naming inns, taverns, villages, etc., after important domestic animals, which may be the explanation for the name of this dance.

**Records:** Folkraft 1174; World of Fun M109.

**Steps:** Run, slide, skip.

**Formation:** Partners in a longways set of three couples, all facing front of room with lady on her partner's right. For learning, number the couples 1, 2, and 3. (Couple 1 is nearest front of room.)

**Timing and Rhythm:** One beat per step (4-beat introduction on M109).

**PATTERN:**

PART I:   **Forward a Double and Back.** With right hands joined about shoulder high, take 4 light running steps forward (beginning R), and 4 steps backward. (A variation is done with 2 running steps, R, L, forward, then in place one "three," R-L-R, then backward L, R, L-R-L.)

Repeat **Forward a Double and Back.**

**Slides.** Partners face each other, join both hands about shoulder high. The first couple slides sidewards 4 steps toward front of room.

Then couple two follows with 4 slide steps.

Next, couple three slides up 4 steps.

**Turn Single.** All release hands and turn individually to the right in place with 4 steps.

Repeat **Slides,** partners again joining both hands, do 4 sliding steps to return to original position in reverse order beginning with couple number three, then two, and one.

Repeat **Turn Single.**

PART II:   **Siding.** Partners face, move forward a double, exchanging places by moving diagonally to the right and passing left shoulders. All turn left, do forward a double back to place, passing right shoulders. It's helpful if partners maintain eye-to-eye contact.

Repeat **Siding.**

**Diagonals.** The first man (1) and last lady (3) change places with 4 sliding steps, passing back to back and leading with right shoulders.

The first lady (1) and last man (3) do the same, leading with left shoulders.

Then the second man (2) and lady (2) change places with sliding steps.

Repeat **Turn Single.**

Repeat **Diagonals,** returning to position by repeating the action in the same order.

Repeat **Turn Single.**

PART III:   **Arming.** Partners face, link right elbows, turn CW with 8 steps. Then link left elbows and turn CCW with 8 steps.

**Men's Hey.** Couple one faces couple two while couples two and three face up toward front of room. With 16 skipping steps the men dance a figure-8, while the ladies stand in place. The first and second men start by skipping out to own left. The third man waits about two counts and then moves out to his right to begin his figure-8, letting the first man pass in front of him as they meet in the center of the 8. They end in starting position.

**Ladies Hey.** The ladies dance a figure-8 exactly the same way, while the men stand in place. As they complete the figure-8, on the last four steps, the men **Turn Single** and honor their partner.

## RHYTHMIC LEARNING CUES:

I:   **Forward a Double and Back.**   Forward, 2, 3, 4; back, 2, 3, 4.

Forward, 2, 3, 4; back, 2, 3, 4.

**Slides.**   One, slide, 3, 4.

Two, slide, 3, 4.

Three, slide, 3, 4.

**Turn Single.**   Turn, right, 3, 4.

**Slides.**   Three, slide, 3, 4.

Two, slide, 3, 4.

One, slide, 3, 4.

**Turn Single.**   Turn, 2, 3, 4.

II:   **Siding.**   Side, 2, 3, 4; back, 2, 3, 4.

Side, 2, 3, 4; back, 2, 3, 4.

**Diagonals.**   Man, one, slide, slide.

Man, three, slide, slide.

Man, two, change, places.

**Turn Single.**   Turn, 2, 3, 4.

Repeat **Diagonals** and **Turn Single.**

III:   **Arming.**   Arm, right, . . . . . . . . 7, place.

Arm, left, . . . . . . . . 7, place.

**Men's Hey.**   Skip, . . . . . . . . . . . . . skip.

**Ladies' Hey.**   Skip, . . . . . . . . . . . . skip.

On the last 4 counts of the **Ladies'**

**Hey,** the men **Turn Single.**

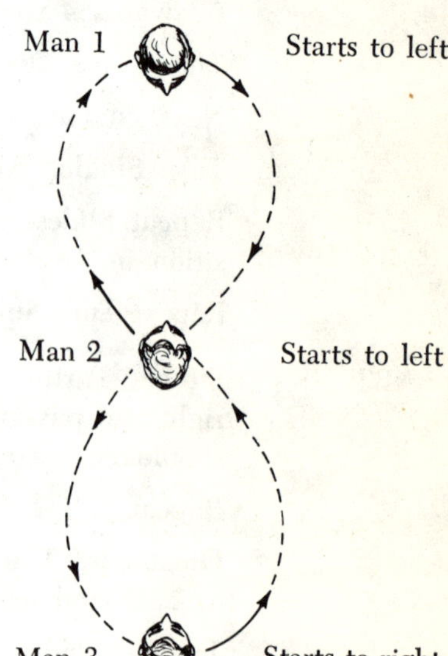

# BOSSA NOVA AMERICAN

An American novelty dance which can be done as a couple dance or individually. Source: "Buzz" Glass.

Record: Columbia 4-42661 (Eyde Gorme).

**Steps:** Two-step, Charleston, point, step.

**Formation:** Free formation, partners facing. Lady does opposite footwork throughout. For learning, it helps if all men face front of the room and hold partner's hands.

**Timing and Rhythm:** One beat per step (long 21-beat introduction, starting the sideward two-step one beat before the vocal on C 4-42661).

## PATTERN:

PART I:    Moving to man's left, both do one two-step sideward (step, close, step, pause), man begins L, lady R. The pause can be done as a touch with the trailing foot.

Moving to man's right, both do one two-step sideward, man begins R, lady L.

Repeat all of Part I.

PART II:    Man moving forward (lady backward), both do one two-step, man begins L, lady R.

Man moving backward (lady forward), both do one two-step, man begins R, lady L.

Repeat all of Part II.

PART III:    Both do two Charleston steps (step, point, step, point), man beginning by stepping forward on L then pointing R forward, lady beginning by stepping R backward and pointing L backward.

PART IV:    Both do a six-step cross and point pattern: man steps forward on L, points R to right side, crosses R in front of L and steps on it, points L to left side, crosses L over R and steps on it, points R to right side. Lady using opposite footwork begins by stepping R backward, pointing L, and crossing L behind R, etc.

Both end with 3 light stamps in place (man R, L, R; lady L, R, L).

## RHYTHMIC LEARNING CUES:

*(Man's cues; lady opposite footwork)*

I:  *(To left)*  L R L R  Side, close, side, touch.      III: *(In place)*  L R R L  Forward, point, back, point,

  *(To right)*  R L R L  Side, close, side, touch.      "  L R R L  Forward, point, back, point.

  *(Repeat I)*

II.  *(Fwd)*  L R L R  Step, close, step, touch.      IV: *(In place)*  L R R L L R  Forward, point, cross, point, cross, point,

  *(Bwd)*  R L R L  Step, close, step, touch.      "  R L R  Stamp, stamp, stamp.

  *(Repeat II)*

# CHERKASSIYA
(Tcherkessia)

ISRAELI

Pronounced:  Chair-ka-SEE-yah

This dance apparently was brought to Israel by Russian immigrants. It has several parts, but it is easy to do and is most enjoyable. Learned from Fred Berk.

Records:  RCA Victor EPA4140; Educ. Dance Record. FD-3; Israel Music Foundation 116B; Tikva T106.

**Steps:**  Grapevine, step-hop, swivel, kick, buzz-step.

**Formation:**  No partners, closed single circle, all facing center, hands joined. Leader can call the sequence as he desires, or substitute improvised steps or hand movements.

**Timing and Rhythm:**  Four beats per grapevine step (8-beat introduction on RCA EPA4140).

**PATTERN:**

| | |
|---|---|
| CHORUS: | Moving to the left (CW), do 4 grapevine steps, beginning R (step R across L with a stamp, step L to left, step R behind L, step L to left). |
| PART I: | **Cherkassiya.** Moving right (CCW), step to the right with R. Step L behind R and bend both knees.<br>Repeat this for a total of 8 times. |
| CHORUS: | **Repeat Chorus.** |
| PART II: | **Horse Trot.** 8 step-hops to the right (CCW) beginning on R. |
| CHORUS: | **Repeat Chorus.** |
| PART III: | **Swivels.** Keep both feet together, move toes to the right and then heels to the right. This is done continuously 8 times. |
| CHORUS: | **Repeat Chorus.** |
| PART IV: | **Forward Scissors.** In place, kick right foot forward, then left foot. Do this 8 times. |
| CHORUS: | **Repeat Chorus.** |
| PART V: | **Backward Scissors.** Repeat Part IV, kicking backward. |
| CHORUS: | **Repeat Chorus.** |
| PART VI: | **Choo-Choo Train.** Moving right, do 8 buzz-steps, shuffling the feet, keeping R in lead. |

**RHYTHMIC LEARNING CUES:**

CHORUS:     *(To CW)*

     R   L   R   L   R   L   R   L
Cross, side, behind, side; cross, side, behind, side.

     R   L   R   L   R   L   R   L
Cross, side, behind, side; cross, side, behind, side.

SEQUENCE:     Chorus. Cherkassiya. Chorus. Horse trot. Chorus. Swivels.

Chorus. Forward Scissors. Chorus. Backward Scissors. Chorus.

Choo-Choo Train.

# COTTON-EYED JOE

American

There are many versions of the figures done to this traditional American fiddle tune.

Records:  World of Fun M118; Imperial 1045B; Educ. Dance Record. FD-3.

**Steps:**  Two-step, chug, heel and toe.

**Formation:**  Partners facing, double circle formation, men with backs to center of circle, two-hand position, for learning; otherwise free formation and closed position. Lady uses opposite footwork throughout.

**Timing and Rhythm:**  Two beats per two-step (8-beat introduction on I 1045).

**PATTERN:**

PART I:  Man touches L heel out to left side, then points L toe in front of R foot (lady R heel and toe).

Moving CCW, both do one two-step (step, close, step, pause), man begins L, lady R.

Repeat all above in reverse direction, man beginning R, lady L.

PART II:  Release hands, partners turn away from each other (man to left, lady to right), each making a small circle in 3 two-steps. End facing partners and taking three quick stamps in place.

PART III:  Partners facing, take four chug steps (to man's left, woman's right). Then do four chug steps in reverse direction.

PART IV:  In closed position, take four two-steps, turning CW and moving CCW around the room.

**RHYTHMIC LEARNING CUES:**

*(Man begins L, lady R)*

I:  *(To CCW)*  Heel, and, toe, and, step, close, step.

*(To CW)*  Heel, and, toe, and, step, close, step.

II:  *(Circle)*  Two-step, 2 . , 3 . .

Stamp, stamp, stamp.

III:  *(To CCW)*  Chug, 2 . , 3 . , 4 . .

*(To CW)*  Chug, 2 . , 3 . , 4 . .

IV:  *(Turn)*  Two-step, 2 . , 3 . , 4 . .

**AS A MIXER:**  In Part IV do only 3 two-steps, then men move ahead to forward lady to repeat the dance.

**Styling:**  Lively and flirtatious, especially in Part III, where the partners should take every advantage of the chug steps to do some fancy stepping. This is the series chug step, which allows plenty of time for embellishment. In some groups, Part I is done with considerable elevation and covering a lot of space. Part II is more restrained, with the arms down at the sides. Part III, with the girls swishing skirts, etc. and the men doing their high-stepping, can be very showy.

# CIULEANDRA ROMANIAN

Pronounced:  Chool-YAHN-drah

There are many dances in Romania called Ciuleandra. This dance, from southern Romania, the region of Oltenia, was introduced into the United States by Mihai David of Los Angeles. Described as learned from Lillian Sutor of Atlanta, Georgia at the 1973 Tennessee Octoberfest Folk Dance Camp.

Record:  Folklore Dances of Romania FLDR-A.

**Steps:**  Step, grapevine, stamp.

**Formation:**  No partners, broken single circle, all facing center, arms in shoulder hold position, leader at the right end.

**Timing and Rhythm:**  One beat per step (32 beat introduction on FLDR-A).

**PATTERN:**

PART I:    Step R to the right, sway to the right with a slight bend in R knee.

Step L to the left, sway to the left with a slight bend in the L knee.

Repeat the step, sway to the right, and the step, sway to the left.

Step R heel forward towards center, close L to R while stepping down on the full R foot.

Step L heel forward towards center, close R to L while stepping down on the full L foot.

Step R slightly to the right, raise the bent L knee forward, step on L slightly to the left, close R to L with a stamp (no weight).

Moving left (CW) do 3½ grapevine steps, beginning with R (cross, side, behind, side; cross, side, behind, side; cross, side, behind, side; cross, side). Close R to L, pause.

Repeat Part I six more times (total 7).

PART II:    **Sevens.**  Moving to the right (CCW), step on R to the right, step on L behind R, step on R to the right, step on L behind R, step on R to the right, step on L behind R, step on R to the right, close L to a R with a stamp (no weight).

Repeat "Sevens" to the left (CW) with opposite footwork.

Repeat "Sevens" to the right, and to the left.

**Ones and Threes.**  Step on R to the right, close L to R with a stamp (no weight); step on L to the left, close R to L with a stamp (no weight). Moving right (CCW), step on R to the right, step on L behind R, step on R to the right, close L to R with a stamp (no weight).

Repeat "Ones and Threes" to the left with opposite footwork.

Repeat "Ones and Threes" again, starting **first to** the right, then to the left.

Repeat Part II, ending the whole dance with a repeat of "Sevens" to the right, left, right, and left.

**RHYTHMIC LEARNING CUES:**

I:    (*In place*)
      R     L     R     L
Step, sway, step, sway, step, sway, step, sway.

(*To center*)
      R  R  L  L  R  L  L  R
Heel, flat, heel, flat, step, lift, step, stamp.

(*CW*)
      R   L   R   L   R   L   R   L
Cross, side, behind, side, cross, side, behind, side.

      R   L   R   L   R   L   R
Cross, side, behind, side, cross, side, close, pause.

(*Repeat I - total 7*),

II:    (*To CCW*)
      R   L   R   L   R   L   R   L
Step, behind, step, behind, step, behind, step, stamp.

(*To CW*)
      L   R   L   R   L   R   L   R
Step, behind, step, behind, step, behind, step, stamp.

(*Repeat to CCW and to CW*).

(*To CCW*)
      R   L   L   R   R   L   R   L
Step, stamp, step, stamp, step, behind, step, stamp.

(*To CW*)
      L   R   R   L   L   R   L   R
Step, stamp, step, stamp, step, behind, step, stamp.

(*Repeat to CCW and to CW*).

(*Repeat II, end with "Sevens" to CCW, CW, CCW, CW*).

**Styling:** Although there is a strong tendency to sway during the introduction, this should be restrained to a very subtle movement, or perhaps slight knee bends on the beat. Many groups shout "Ho! Sha, SHAH, shah, SHAH!" during the last 4 beats before the grapevine in Part I (along with the singer on the record). The music gradually speeds up, the dancers accelerate their nimble feet. The velocity gets exciting!

# D'HAMMERSCHMIEDSG'SELLN

GERMAN

Pronounced:  D-HAH-mehr-shmeeds-g-ZEHL-n

"The blacksmith's apprentice" was originally a dance for men only. Introduced by Vyts Beliajus, it has proved to be a good 2-couple dance.

Record:  Folkraft 1485 × 45B, Folkraft LP5.

**Steps:**  Step-hop, waltz.

**Formation:**  Four dancers (preferably 2 couples), partners facing each other across the other couple, so each couple will clap hands between the other couple.

**Timing and Rhythm:**  Hand-clapping, one beat per clap; step-hops, 3 beats per step-hop (12-beat introduction on Folkraft LP5).

**HAND CLAPPING:**   (6 counts)

1. Clap hands on own thighs (bend the knees a little on this clap and slap the thighs lightly).
2. Clap hands on own waist.
3. Clap own hands together.
4. Clap opposite person's right hand.
5. Clap opposite person's left hand.
6. Clap opposite person's both hands.

In order to coordinate the four dancers' clapping, one couple must start the entire 6-count clap pattern on the count of 1. The other couple waits, and on the count of 4 begins their 6-count clap pattern, by clapping thighs. The clap pattern is done 8 times during each hand clapping.

Starting Position

**PATTERN:**

**Clapping: Repeat Hand Clapping.**

PART   I:     **Circle.** The 4 join hands and step-hop, circling left (CW) with 8 step-hops. Then reverse the circling, doing 8 step-hops right (CCW).

**Clapping: Repeat Hand Clapping.**

PART   II:     **Star.** The 4 join right hands forming a right hand star, and step-hop CW around, 8 step-hops. Reverse, 8 step hops CCW.

**Clapping: Repeat Hand Clapping.**

PART III:     **Waltz.** Take partner and waltz anywhere. Or, in Part III all dancers on the floor can join hands in a big circle and do 8 step-hops left (CW), and 8 step-hops right (CCW).

**LEARNING CUES:**

|  |  |  |
|---|---|---|
| **Clap Pattern:** | *(Own)* | Thigh, waist, own. |
|  | *(Ptnr)* | Right, left, both. |
| **Sequence:** |  | Clap. Circle. Clap. Star. Clap. Waltz. |

# FADO BLANQUITO

Portuguese-Brazilian

Pronounced:  FAH-doe Blahn-KEE-toh

This dance has been attributed to Spanish, Portuguese, and even Brazilian origins. At any rate, the music and the dance are both fun.

Records:  Folkraft 1173; RCA Victor LPM 1620; Educ. Dance Record. FD-4.

**Steps:**  Schottische, run, jump.

**Formation:**  Partners, single closed circle, all facing center, lady on partner's right, all hands joined.

**Timing and Rhythm:**  One beat per running step (8-beat introduction on FD-4).

### PATTERN:

PART I:   Circling left (CW), and beginning with L, all take 16 running steps.
Then circle right (CCW) with 16 running steps.

PART II:   Partners face, join right hands, with elbows bent and fingers pointed up, "sway" to right, left, right, and left by shifting the weight each time.

With right hands still joined and left hand behind back, do 3 schottische steps around each other, beginning R (step, step, step, hop). These are short steps and you should end facing the lady on your left, your corner lady.

Join left hands with corner and repeat the 3 schottische steps turning and ending facing partner.

Repeat the 3 schottische steps with partner, and again with corner.

All join hands around the circle, facing center, do swaying balance to right and to left, and stamp 3 times in place (R-L-R), and pause.

PART III:   Single circle all facing center, hands joined. Jump in place on both feet, then while hopping on R swing L across in front of R. Again jump in place on both feet, then hop on L while swinging R across.

Jump in place, and then jump again turning half-way to right, backs to center. All join hands again.

Repeat the above ending with all facing in, hands joined.

Slowly take 4 walking steps to center, raising hands. Walk backward 4 steps, lowering hands.

Repeat all of Part III.

**RHYTHMIC LEARNING CUES:**

I:      *(To CW)*    L         16
                    Run, run . . . . . . . . . . . run.

       *(To CCW)*    R        16
                    Run, run . . . . . . . . . . . run.

II:    *(Face ptnr)*    R    L    R    L
                    Sway, sway, sway, sway.

      *(Right hand)*    R        L        R
                    Partner, 2, 3, hop; step, 2, 3, hop; step, 2, 3, hop.

      *(Left hand)*    L        R        L
                    Corner, 2, 3, hop; step, 2, 3, hop; step, 2, 3, hop.

      *(Right hand)*    R        L        R
                    Partner, 2, 3, hop; step, 2, 3, hop; step, 2, 3, hop.

      *(Left hand)*    L        R        L
                    Corner, 2, 3, hop; step, 2, 3, hop; step, 2, 3, hop.

      *(Face center)*    R    L    R    L    R
                    Sway, sway, stamp, stamp, stamp.

III.   *(Face center)*    L       R
                    Jump, swing, jump, swing.

      *(Place, turn)*    Jump, jump.

      *(Face wall)*    L       R
                    Jump, swing, jump, swing.

      *(Place, turn)*    Jump, jump.

      *(To center)*    Step, in, raise, hands.

      *(Bwds)*    Step, back, hands, down.

    *(Repeat III)*

# HARMONICA



Fred Berk, the American authority on Israeli dances, says that a folk dance is one that three generations dance together. In Israel, Harmonica has become such a dance, with everyone joining in the joyful spirit of the dance. Choreographed by Dvora Lapson.

**Records:** Folk Dancer MH1091; Folkraft F1009; Arzi A-2004.

**Steps:** Grapevine, step-hop, leap, run.

**Formation:** No partners, closed single circle, all facing somewhat right, hands joined.

**Timing and Rhythm:** One beat per step in grapevine steps (16-beat introduction on FD MH1091).

**PATTERN:**

PART I:  Moving right (CCW), do one grapevine step (step L across R, step R to right, step L behind R, step R to right).

Still moving CCW, step-hop on L, then step-hop on R.

Repeat Part I three more times (total 4).

PART II:  **Harmonica step.** Facing center, step L across and in front of R (body turning a little right) step back in place on R. Bring L back and step in place alongside R (facing center again), hop on L. (Cross, back, step, hop, is one Harmonica step, done in 4 counts. Note that a Harmonica step to the right, starts with L). In all the Harmonica steps, clap own hands at about eye level on the count of 1, as one steps the first step across.

Next, do one Harmonica step to the left (step R across in front of L, step in place on L, step R back alongside L, hop on R).

Now, do one more Harmonica step to the right. Then turning to the left, do 2 step-hops (R-hop, L-hop), moving CW.

Repeat all of Part II, reversing directions and using opposite footwork.

PART III:  (Release joined hands, pull circle closer together, and place hands on neighbors' near shoulders, in shoulder position).

Lightly leap sideward on L, and swing R across L, then leap sideward on R and swing L across R.

Moving left (CW) around the circle, take 4 running steps, beginning L.

Repeat Part III three more times (total 4).

**RHYTHMIC LEARNING CUES:**

I:     *(To CCW)*     
L  L  R  L  R  L  L  R  R
Cross, step, behind, step; left, hop, right, hop.

         *(Repeat I, total 4)*

II:    *(Harmonica)*    
L  R  L  L
Cross, place, back, hop.

                  
R  L  R  R
Cross, place, back, hop.

                  
L  R  L  L
Cross, place, back, hop.

   *(To CW)*      
R  R  L  L
Step, hop, step, hop.

         *(Repeat II, but with opposite directions and footwork)*

III:   *(To CW)*     
L  R  R  L  L  R  L  R
Leap, swing, leap, swing, run, run, run, run.

         *(Repeat III, total 4)*

Israeli

# KALVELIS



Pronounced:  Kahl-VAY-lis

This is a typical European "occupational" folk dance. The name means "The Little Smith" and the clapping of the hands suggests the hammer and anvil. The sequence sometimes differs—this one makes a nice mixer.

Records:  Folk Dancer MH1016; Folkraft 1418 and 1051; Educ. Dance Record. FD-3; World of Fun M101.

**Steps:**  Polka, stamp, skip.

**Formation:**  Partners, closed single circle, all facing center, lady on partner's right, all hands joined.

**Timing and Rhythm:**  Two beats per polka, and one beat per clap (4-beat introduction on F 1418).

**PATTERN:**

PART I:    **Circling.**  Moving right (CCW), all do 7 polka steps (hop, step, close, step), beginning with a hop on L.

In place, stamp 3 times (L, R, L).

Moving left (CW), do 7 polka steps, beginning with a hop on L.

In place, stamp 3 times (L, R, L). End facing partners, still in single circle.

CHORUS:    Partners facing, clap own hands 4 times, alternating clapping right hand down on the left hand which is held parallel to the floor, then left hand on the right held parallel to the floor.

Partners hook right elbows and do a half turn in 2 polka steps (or a full turn with 4 skipping steps).

Partners repeat the clapping pattern, then hook left elbows and do a half turn back to place. End facing center of circle.

Repeat the clapping, right elbow, clapping, and left elbow turns to complete entire chorus.

PART II:   **Center and Back.**  Ladies do 3 polka steps toward center of the circle beginning with a hop on L (while men in place clap hands); ladies stamp 3 times (L, R, L) while turning right, and return to place with 3 polka steps ending with 3 stamps (L, R, L), turning right to face the center again.

Repeat Part II, men doing the 3 polkas in toward the center, 3 stamps, 3 polkas back to place and final stamps. End facing partners.

CHORUS:    **Repeat Chorus.** End facing partners.

PART III:  **Grand Right and Left.**  Do a Grand-Right-and-Left for the time it takes to do 16 polka steps, men moving CCW, ladies CW, around the circle, to the 16th person, your new partner.

Or do the Grand Right and Left for 8 polka counts, to the 8th person, with whom take shoulder-waist position and polka freely around the room, 8 polka steps.

CHORUS:    **Repeat Chorus.** End facing center.

**RHYTHMIC LEARNING CUES:**

I:    *(To CCW)*    Polka . . . . . . . polka, stamp, stamp, stamp.

    *(To CW)*    Polka . . . . . . polka, stamp, stamp, stamp.

Chorus:    Clap, clap, clap, clap.

*(CW)*    Turn, half, way, around.

Clap, clap, clap, clap.

*(CCW)*    Turn, half, way, around.

*(Repeat Chorus)*

II:    *(To center)*    Ladies, polka, in, stamp, stamp, stamp.

*(Back)*    Ladies, polka, back, stamp, stamp, stamp.

*(To center)*    Men, polka, in, stamp, stamp, stamp.

*(Back)*    Men, polka, back, stamp, stamp, stamp.

**Chorus.**

III:    *(Polka)*    Grand-Right-and-Left . . . . . . . . 16.

**Chorus.**

Vyts Beliajus introduced and popularized many Lithuanian dances, including this lively one.

# KOROBUSHKA

**Pronounced:**  Koh-ROH-boosh-ka

This folk dance about a "peddler's pack" was supposedly originated in this country by a group of Russian immigrants around the turn of the century. Source: Michael and Mary Ann Herman.

**Records:**  Folk Dancer MH1059; Educ. Dance Record. FD-3; World of Fun M108.

**Steps:**  Schottische, step-hop, walk.

**Formation:**  Partners, double circle, men on inside with backs to center, facing ladies, both hands joined.

**Timing and Rhythm:**  One beat per step (8-beat introduction on FD MH1059).

**PATTERN:**

PART I:     Both moving away from center of circle, take one schottische step (step, step, step, hop), man stepping L forward, lady R backward.

Both move back toward center with another schottische step, man begins R, lady L.

Do a third schottische step away from center, man L, lady R.

Both hop 3 times on supporting foot (man L, lady R) while pointing other toe forward, then to side, then closing to the supporting foot, man clicks heels together. (Point: see p. 10).

PART II:    Release joined hands, each does a schottische step sideward to own right, beginning R. Return to face each other with a schottische, beginning L.

Join right hands and step-hop forward to partner, then step-hop backward away from partner.

Still holding right hands, change places with partner with 3 walking steps.

Release hands and repeat all of Part II, ending in your starting position, man's back to center.

**RHYTHMIC LEARNING CUES:**

I:              *(Man begins L, lady R)*

    *(To wall)*      Step, 2, 3, hop.

    *(To center)*    Step, 2, 3, hop.

    *(To wall)*      Step, 2, 3, hop.

    *(In place)*     Point, side, together.

II:       *(Own right)*    Right, 2, 3, hop.

    *(Own left)*     Left, 2, 3, hop.

In, back.

Change, 2, 3.

*(Repeat II)*

Ukrainian (Russia)

# KUMA ECHA

Israeli

**Pronounced:** KOO-ma EH-kha

Rivka Sturman composed this dance to a lively Hebrew melody.

**Records:** Folk Dancer MH1150; Folkraft 1431; Educ. Dance Record FD-4; Tikva T-106.

**Steps:** Schottische, grapevine, run.

**Formation:** No partners, closed single circle, all facing center, hands joined.

**Timing and Rhythm:** One beat per step (16-count introduction on FD MH1150).

## PATTERN:

**PART I:**    Moving forward toward center, take one schottische step (R, L, R, hop).

Backwards to place, take one schottische step (L, R, L, hop).

Moving left (CW), do 2 grapevine steps, (step R across L, step L to the left, step R behind L, step L to the left).

Repeat Part I.

**PART II:**    Changing direction and all moving right (CCW), take 2 running steps forward (R, L).

Then still holding hands and moving the same CCW direction, turn left to face CW, and run backwards 2 steps (R, L).

Continue in the same CCW direction, alternating forward 2 runs and backwards 2 runs for a total of 16 running steps. End facing center.

**PART III:**    Moving forward toward center, take 4 walking steps (R, L, R, L).

Then moving gradually backward, stamp R in front of L, step on L in place, step backwards on R, step on L beside R. Do this 3 times altogether, to expand circle to original size.

## RHYTHMIC LEARNING CUES:

```
                              R    L    R    R
          I:    (To center)   Step, step, step, hop.

                              L    R    L    L
               (Bwd)          Step, step, step, hop.

                              R    L    R    L    R    L    R    L
              (To CW)         Cross, side, behind, side; cross, side, behind, side.


                (Repeat I)


                              R    L    R    L    R    L    R    L
         II:    (To CCW)      Fwd, run; bwd, run; fwd, run; bwd, run.


                (Repeat II)


                              R    L    R    L
        III:    (To center)   Step, step, step, step.

                              R    L    R    L
               (Bwd)          Stamp, step, step, step.

                              R    L    R    L
               (Bwd)          Stamp, step, step, step.

                              R    L    R    L
               (Bwd)          Stamp, step, step, step.
```

# LECH LECH LAMIDBAR                                        Israeli

Pronounced:  LEKH LEKH Lah-mid-BAHR

According to Fred Berk, from whom this was learned, this is an old folk dance set to a melody composed by Argon. The words mean "Let Us Go Into the Desert."

Records:  MH 1093; Israel Music Foundation LP 118; IMF 2002; UNI 33-107.

**Steps:**  Step, leap, jump, grapevine, step-close, hop.

**Formation:**  No partners, closed single circle, all facing center, hands joined in basic line position.

**Timing and Rhythm:**  One beat per walk, leap or jump (16 beat introduction on MH1093).

**PATTERN:**

PART I:     Moving sideward to the right (CCW), leap lightly to the right on R, step on L across in front of R, step on R beside L, pause.

Moving sideward to the left (CW), take two step-closes beginning L, (step L, close R; step L, close R, not taking weight on last close).

Repeat all of Part I three more times (total 4).

PART II:     In place, jump on both feet, lightly kick L forward, jump on both feet, lightly kick R forward.

Moving left (CW) do one grapevine step (step R across L, step L to the left, step R behind L, step L to the left).

Repeat all of Part II three more times (total 4).

PART III:     Step R forward toward center of circle while raising joined hands high, step back to place on L while lowering hands, step R beside L, pause.

Moving sideward to the left (CW) take two step-closes beginning L (not taking weight on last close).

Repeat all of Part III one more time (total 2).

PART IV:     Moving left (CW) do a 7-step grapevine (step R across L, step L to the left, step R behind L, step L to the left, step R across L, step L to the left, step R behind L) and hop on R.

Moving right (CCW) repeat the 7-step grapevine by stepping L across R, ending with a hop on L.

Repeat all of Part IV one more time (total 2).

**RHYTHMIC LEARNING CUES:**

I:    (*To right*)    Leap, cross, close, pause.
        R   L    R

(*To left*)    Step, close, step, touch.
     L   R   L    R

(*Repeat I, total 4.*)

II:    (*In place*)    Jump, kick, jump, kick.
           L      R

(*To left*)    Cross, side, behind, side.
     R   L    R    L

(*Repeat II, total 4.*)

III:    (*To center*)    Forward, back, close, pause.
       R    L   R

(*To left*)    Step, close, step, touch.
     L   R   L    R

(*Repeat III, total 2.*)

IV:    (*To left*)    Cross, side, behind, side, cross, side, behind, hop.
     R  L   R   L   R   L   R    R

(*To right*)    Cross, side, behind, side, cross, side, behind, hop.
     L   R   L   R   L   R   L    L

(*Repeat IV, total 2.*)

**Styling:**  The feeling of the dance is light, with considerable lift or elevation. The changes of direction in Part I (from right movement, to left) and in Part III (from forward movement, to left) should be quite crisp. Many groups do not hold hands in Part I, but each dancer claps own hands on the "closes." According to Israeli folk dancer Israel Yakovee, Part III is done by many groups thus: facing center, stamp R sideward to the right, pause; stamp L sideward to the left, pause; then step R fwd toward center of circle while raising joined hands high, step to place on L while lowering hands, step R beside L, pause.

# LIMBO ROCK

American

This novelty dance for couples, based on a recent popular hit tune, was composed by Henry "Buzz" Glass.

Record:  Challenge 59131.

**Steps:**  Step, two-step.

**Formation:**  Partners, free formation. The dance is sometimes done as a mixer, in which case the couples form a double circle, all facing counterclockwise, skater's position.

**Timing and Rhythm:**  One beat per step (brief 3-note introduction on C 59131, 2 beats).

**PATTERN:**

PART I:  **Two-steps** (Rhythm:  1, 2, 3, pause; 4 beats).

Step forward 16 two-steps (modified with knee bends to achieve a relaxed but controlled bounce: step fwd on L, step on R beside L, step slightly fwd on L foot, pause. Repeat R, etc.). The 16 two-steps are done only in the initial sequence. In the repeats, only 4 two-steps are done.

End by dropping hands, and both partners turn away from center of room to face the wall—man is behind his partner.

PART II:  **The Chase** (Rhythm:  slow, slow, quick, quick, quick, pause; 8 beats).

Step forward L (slow), step back R (slow), then three steps essentially in place L, R, L (quick, quick, quick) while turning to left and both face the center of the room (pause).

Repeat with opposite footwork, R forward (slow), L back (slow), R, L, R (quick, quick, quick) turning right to face the wall again (pause).

Repeat the *Chase* again starting L, and then starting R.

End both facing forward (CCW), and in original skater's position.

PART III:  **Heels** (Rhythm:  1 ah, 2 ah, 3 ah, 4 ah; 8 beats.)

Moving right:  bring L over in front of R and somewhat to the right of R and step on the L heel (count 1), step sideward to the right with R (ah), again on L heel (count 2), again sideward R (ah), again L heel (3), sideward R (ah), again L heel (count 4); end by swinging R around and over in front of L and somewhat to the left of L (ah).

Moving left:  (reverse footwork) having brought R around, step on R heel (count 1), step sideward L (ah), again R heel (2), sideward L (ah), again R heel (3), sideward L (ah), and again R heel (count 4); end with a pause (ah), L free and ready to start Part I again.

Repeat from the beginning. Remember, do only 4 two-steps in Part I.

**RHYTHMIC LEARNING CUES:**

I:      **Two-steps.**    Left, close, left; right, close, right;

*(two-steps—16 initially, then 4).*


II:     **Chase.**    *(To wall)*    L    R    L    R    L
Slow, slow, quick, quick, quick, and.

*(To center)*    R    L    R    L    R
Slow, slow, quick, quick, and.

*(Repeat II)*


III:    **Heels.**    *(To right)*    L    R    L    R    L    R    L    R
Heel, ah, heel, ah, heel, ah, heel, swing.

*(To left)*    R    L    R    L    R    L    R
Heel, ah, heel, ah, heel, ah, heel, and.

**NOTE:** Mary Ann Herman has developed another interesting pattern, starting with the *Chase*, then *Heels*, then *Two-steps*. The *Chase* is somewhat different: Rhythm: 1, 2, 3, 4, 5, 6, 7, 8. Position: as described above for Part II. Step forward on L (count 1), step on R in place (2), step back on L (3), step on R in place (4), step forward on L (5), step R in place (6), step L (7); finish by pivoting left on L to face center of room (8). Continue with reverse footwork, finishing by pivoting right to face out. Continue once more out and once more in.

# MAYIM

ISRAELI

**Pronounced:** MAH-yim

A good circle dance for all ages. "Mayim" means "water!" and is one of the dances that has become so well known in Israel that it has become like a traditional folk dance, according to Fred Berk.

**Records:** Folkraft 1108; Israeli 114; World of Fun M119; Tikva T106, and others.

**Steps:** Grapevine, walk, hop, point.

**Formation:** No partners, closed single circle, all facing center, hands joined.

**Timing and Rhythm:** One beat per step (40-beat introduction on Israeli 114, 8-beat on M119).

**PATTERN:**

PART I:  Moving left (CW), do 4 grapevine steps (step R across L, step L to the left, step R behind L, step L to left).

PART II:  All move to center with 4 walking steps, raising joined hands high and singing, "Mayim, mayim, mayim, mayim!"

Walk backwards with 4 steps, lowering hands.

Repeat walking in and back.

PART III:  Face left, still holding hands and starting on R run to the left 4 steps. (Finish facing center on the 4th step.)

Step on R, then hop on R while pointing L in front of R, then hop on R while pointing L to left side. Continue the hop-points to front, side, front, side, front and side.

Quickly change feet by stepping on L, then hopping on L while pointing R to front, to right side, etc. for total of 8 hop-points. While switching feet, release hands, and clap own hands in front of forehead every time you point R in front.

**RHYTHMIC LEARNING CUES:**

I:    (To CW)

R    L    R    L    R    L    R    L
Cross, side, behind, side; cross, side, behind, side.

"

R    L    R    L    R    L    R    L
Cross, side, behind, side; cross, side, behind, side.

II:    (Fwd and bwd)

R                R
In, 2, 3, 4; back, 2, 3, 4.

"

R                R
In, 2, 3, 4; back, 2, 3, 4.

III:    (To CW)

R
Run, 2, 3, 4.

(In place)

R    L    R    L    R    L    R    L
Hop-point, hop-point, hop-point, hop-point.

"

L    R    L    R    L    R    L    R
Hop-clap, hop-clap, hop-clap, hop-clap.

# NEBESKO KOLO                                                    SERBIAN

The name of this dance means "heavenly circle." Dick Crum and the Hermans popularized this dance.

Records: Folk Dancer MH1003; Folkraft 1401; Educ. Dance Record. FD-4. Balkan 513.

**Steps:** Two-step, step, threes, stamp.

**Formation:** No partners, open single circle, all face center, hands joined.

**Timing and Rhythm:** Two beats per two-step (no introduction on FD MH1003).


## PATTERN:

PART I:       Moving to the right (CCW), all take 4 two-steps, starting on R.

Still holding hands, turn and do 4 two-steps to the left (CW).

PART II:      Face center, step forward on R, step back in place on L, step backward on R, in place on L.

Repeat the R forward, L in place, R backward, L in place. (As R is stepped forward and back, the joined hands can be swung forward and back.)

PART III:     Each dancer does 4 "threes" (3 quick steps in place) first to the right, then to the left, to the right, and to the left. End with a sharp stamp with R in place.


## RHYTHMIC LEARNING CUES:

I:     *(To CCW)*     
R  
Two-step, right, 3 . , turn.

*(To CW)*     
R  
Two-step, left, 3 . , 4 . .

II:     *(In place)*     
R     L     R     L  
Forward, place, backward, place.

*(In place)*     
R     L     R     L  
Forward, place, backward, place.

III:     *(In place)*     
R     L     R     L     R  
1-2-3, 1-2-3, 1-2-3, 1-2-3, stamp!

**Styling:** As in most Serbian dances, the steps are small and crisp. The body is held erect, and the bearing is one of pride. In one variation (there are many), Part I is done with 2 two-steps moving right, then continuing right with a R, L, and a "three" (R, L, R) to turn to face CW. Similarly, but with opposite footwork, move to the left. The R, L, following the two-steps in this variation are done with a wide base, leaping slightly, diagonally to the right, then to the left, and reversing this footwork when moving left.

# NEVER ON SUNDAY



This dance has an interesting history. Originally the pattern was taken from one of the basic steps of the Cretan Syrtos "Kritikos" by American folk dancers—some say in Buffalo, some Pittsburgh. The dance, then called "Misirlou," became immensely popular among folk dancers throughout the United States. When the movie "Never on Sunday" became such a big hit, Robert Wiechnick, formerly of Wheeling, West Virginia, and now of New York City, took the basic Misirlou step, elaborated on it, and produced this popular version.

**Records:**  United Arts 234; RCA 47-7769.

**Steps:**  Step, pivot, point or brush.

**Formation:**  No partners, closed single circle, all facing center, hands joined.

**Timing and Rhythm:**  One beat per slow step or 2 quick steps (18-beat introduction, including 4 finger-snap sounds plus 14 musical beats, on RCA 47-7769).

**PATTERN:**

PART I:  **Misirlou step.**  (Rhythm: *slow, slow, quick, quick, quick, pivot, quick, quick, quick, pause, quick, quick, quick, pause.*)

Step on R (*slow*). Pause. Point L toe forward (*slow*), (the point is often done as a brush forward), then swing L around behind R and step on L in back of R (*quick*). Step on R sideward to the right (*quick*). Step on L in front of R (*quick*). Pivot left on L to face directly CW (*pivot*).

Step forward (CW), R, L, R (*quick, quick, quick*) and pause, (L foot ready to step backward) (*pause*).

Step backward (CCW) L, R, L (*quick, quick, quick*), and pause turning to face center.

Repeat Part I.

PART II:  **Triple pivot.**  (Rhythm: *slow, slow, quick, quick, quick, pivot, quick, quick, quick, pivot, quick, quick, quick, pivot, quick, quick, quick, pause, quick, quick, quick, pause.*)

As in Part I, step R, pause, point L, then step L, R, L, (moving CCW), pivot, then moving CW step R, L, R (*slow, slow, quick, quick, quick, pivot, quick, quick, quick*). Again pivot to face CCW (*pivot*).

Moving CCW, step L, R, L (*quick, quick, quick*). Again pivot to face CW (*pivot*).

Moving CW, step R, L, R, pause, and moving backward (CCW) step L, R, L (*quick, quick, quick, pause, quick, quick, quick*), and pause facing center.

Repeat Part II.

PART III:  **Criss-Cross.**  (Rhythm: *slow, slow, quick, quick, quick, pivot, slow, slow, quick, quick, quick, (pause, quick, quick, quick, pause.*)

As in Part I, step R, pause, point L, then step L, R, L, (moving CCW), pivot (to face center) (*slow, slow, quick, quick, quick, pivot*).

Then step R over in front of L and somewhat to the left of L (*slow*), step L over in front of R and somewhat to the right of R (*slow*), turning to face CW. (*Slow, slow.*)

Finish stepping (CW) R, L, R, pause, and stepping backward (CCW) with L, R, L (*quick, quick, quick, pause, quick, quick, quick*) and pause, facing center.

Repeat Part III.

## RHYTHMIC LEARNING CUES:

I:     *(Face center)*

      R      L        L  CCW  L   CW
Step, and, point, and, behind, 2, 3, pivot, forward,

      CCW
2, 3, and, back, 2, 3, and.

*(Repeat I)*

II:    *(Face center)*

      R      L        L  CCW  L   CW
Step, and, point, and, behind, 2, 3, pivot, forward,

        R  CCW        L   CW
2, 3, pivot, forward, 2, 3, pivot, forward, 2, 3,

      CCW
and, back, 2, 3, and.

*(Repeat II)*

III:   *(Face center)*

      R      L        L  CCW  L   R
Step, and, point, and, behind, 2, 3, pivot, criss, and,

      L     CW        CCW
cross, and, forward, 2, 3, and, back, 2, 3, and.

*(Repeat III)*

**Styling:** Movements should be smooth and fluid. Try to avoid exaggeration — keeping the feeling of lightness. Greeks express their joy and pleasure in dancing by hissing, and shouting "Yah-soo" or "Ho-pah." During the introduction on the record, they might snap their fingers before joining hands and beginning the dance. The dance **Misirlou** is also very popular. Use just the Misirlou step as described in Part I, and one of the following records: Columbia 10072-78; Kolo Festival KF804-B; Electra EKL-206.

# ORIJENT
SERBIAN

Pronounced:  Oh-ree-YENT

This dance comes from a group of villages just south of Belgrade, the capitol of both Serbia and Jugoslavia. Originally introduced by Dick Crum, it has become very popular among American folk dancers. Described as taught by Dick Crum at the 1967 East Tennessee State University Octoberfest.

Record: Du-TAM 1001A; KH 101A.

**Steps:**  Step, point.

**Formation:**  No partners, broken single circle or line, hands joined in V-position. When men dance Oriient in separate lines, they use the shoulder hold position.

**Timing and Rhythm:**  One beat per step. In Parts I and III the rhythm is slow, slow, quick, quick, quick, with one beat per slow step, and two beats per 3 quick steps. (No introduction on Du-TAM 1001.)

**PATTERN:**

PART I:  All facing somewhat right and moving right (CCW), point L toe (touching the floor) across R (slow), step on L (slow), step on R forward in LOD (quick), step on L behind R (quick), step R forward in LOD (quick).

Repeat I seven more times (total 8).

PART II:  All facing center, and bending forward at the waist, stretch L leg straight out to the left then step on L; step R across in front of L; step L across in front of R, while straightening up; pause. (This movement forms a semi-circle out to the left and forward toward the center.)

Move straight backward to place with 3 steps, R, L, R, and pause. During this pause, stretch the L leg straight out to the left and shake L foot vigorously, preparatory to stepping on L for the next repeat of Part II. Continue this for each repeat, but on the last repeat do not stretch L leg — just pause, preparatory for Part III.

Repeat II three more times (total 4).

PART III:  Moving just a little toward the center, step L forward 2 or 3 inches (on ball of foot) while swiveling both heels to left but with no weight on R (slow); similarly, step R forward 2 or 3 inches while swiveling both heels to right (slow); again, step L and swivel left (quick); step R and swivel right (quick); step L and swivel left (quick).

Continue moving slightly toward center, but with opposite footwork and swiveling (R, L, R-L-R).

Repeat steps and swivels but moving slightly backwards to place, stepping and swiveling beginning L, (L, R, L-R-L; R, L, R-L-R).

Repeat all of Part III.

**RHYTHMIC LEARNING CUES:**

                                    L    L    R    L    R

I:       (*To CCW*)    Point, step, side, behind, side.

       (*Repeat I, total 8.*)

                                 L     R   L

II:     (*To center*)    Stretch, step, step, and,

                             R    L   R

      (*Bwd*)    back, step, step, and.

       (*Repeat II, total 4.*)

                             L    R    L    R    L

III:    (*To center*)    Swivel, swivel, quick, quick, quick;

                           R    L    R    L    R

     (*To center*)    swivel, swivel, quick, quick, quick.

                           L    R    L    R    L

      (*Bwd*)    Swivel, swivel, quick, quick, quick;

                           R    L    R    L    R

      (*Bwd*)    swivel, swivel, quick, quick, quick.

       (*Repeat III.*)

**Styling:**  As in all Serbian dances, the steps are small, precise, and crisp. Part I is quite bouncy, on the balls of the feet, with a considerable feeling of lift as well as strong forward thrust. On the other hand, Part II feels low, with the body bent until one straightens up. Part III is very relaxed and subtle, with no exaggeration of the swivels.

Serbian "Guslar"—playing the traditional gusle.

# OSLO WALTZ

This old-time dance, introduced by Michael and Mary Ann Herman, is said to be a Scotch-English family waltz, set to a Norwegian folk tune. It is often used as a good-night dance by many groups.

Records: Folk Dancer MH3016.

**Steps:** Waltz-balance, step-draw, waltz.

**Formation:** Partners, single circle, all facing center, lady on her partner's right, all hands joined.

**Timing and Rhythm:** Three beats per waltz step (8-waltz-step introduction on FD MH3016 takes 24 beats).

## PATTERN:

PART I:     All do one waltz-balance step forward (step, rise, step), (man begins L, lady R), and one waltz-balance backward.

The man takes 2 waltz steps (6 small steps) in place as the lady crosses over in front of the man to her right with 2 waltz steps (6 steps) making a full turn to the right, keeping eye contact, as she progresses CCW, and immediately all rejoin hands in a single circle. (It will help a lot if the man uses his strong left arm to help swing the lady from his left to his right hand.)

Repeat Part I three more times (total 4).

PART II:     (Each man faces and joins both hands with the lady now on his right, the 4th lady he has just swung across to his right.) Waltz-balance sidewards to the center of the circle (man begins L, lady R) and away from center.

Release hands and each make a full turn toward center, man turning CCW to left, lady turning CW to right, in 2 waltz steps, end facing partner.

Rejoin both hands and waltz-balance away from center, then towards center.

Release hands and in 2 waltz steps each make a full turn away from center, man turning CW to right, lady turning CCW to left.

PART III:     Resume two-hand position and take two step-draws toward the center (do not take weight on trailing foot after last draw) and do two step-draws away.

Take closed position and do 4 turning (CW) waltz steps around the circle CCW. (Dancers can use the two-hand position and make one complete turn CW with 4 waltz steps.)

## RHYTHMIC LEARNING CUES:

*(Man begins L, lady R)*

I:     *(Face center)*     Balance in, balance out, and turn, the first.
Balance in, balance out, and turn, the next.
Balance in, balance out, and turn, the third.
Balance in, balance out, and turn, the fourth.

II:     *(Face ptnr)*     Balance in, balance out, turn in, to center.
Balance out, balance in, turn away, from center.

III:     *(Face ptnr)*     Step-in, step-draw.
Step-out, step-draw.
Waltz turn, 2 . , 3 . , 4 . .

# PATA PATA



Pronounced:  PAH-ta PAH-ta

Ken Spear, who taught this novelty dance at the 1972 Tennessee Octoberfest Folk Dance Camp, said that he does not know where the dance originated, but this is the version that is so popular in the New York area.

Record:  Reprise 0732.

**Steps:**  Touch, step, kick.

**Formation:**  No partners, free formation. For learning, everyone can face the same direction.

**Timing and Rhythm:**  One beat per step. (After the first note of music, there's a 16 beat introduction on R-0732.)

**PATTERN:**

PART I:    Touch R toe sideward to right, step on R in front of L, touch L toe sideward to left, step on L beside R, both feet together.

PART II:    Swivel both toes apart (keeping heels together) while raising both hands up (palms forward and elbows close to sides).

Swivel both heels apart, while bringing both hands down, close to sides, elbows out.

Swivel both heels together, while raising both hands as before.

Swivel both toes together, lowering the hands and arms.

PART III:    Raise R knee up in front of L knee, touch R foot to floor, raise R knee again, step on R beside L.

PART IV:    Kick L foot forward, step back in place on L, step on R in place, while turning a quarter turn to the right. Step on L in place.

*Repeat the dance, making a quarter turn with each repetition, facing a different wall of the room with each quarter turn.*

**RHYTHMIC LEARNING CUES:**

I:              R    R    L    L
               Touch, step, touch, close.

II:   (*Swivel*)   apart  apart  tgth.  tgth.
                   Toes, heels, heels, toes.

III:            R    R    R    R
               Knee, touch, knee, close.

IV:             L    L    R    L
               Kick, step, turn, step.

**Styling:**  Jazz-dance styling is highly appropriate for this dance, meaning that one should use strong movements of the head, shoulders, torso, hips, and knees, and freedom of expression — i.e. — loosen up!

# PUT YOUR LITTLE FOOT



(American Varsouvianna)

There are many variations of this old-time dance which was very popular in the Southwestern United States. It was often pictured in Western movies. The dance is based on the mazurka which was once a favorite dance step of Poland and other European countries. Some believe that the Mexicans learned this dance from the Polish nobility in court, and it then spread into the Southwestern United States.

**Records:** Folk Dancer MH3016; Folkraft 1034 and 1165; Old Timer 8077; Windsor 7615B.

**Steps:** Varsouvianna, varsovienne.

**Formation:** Partners, in free formation or in double circle, all facing counterclockwise, in varsovienne position.

**Timing and Rhythm:** One beat per step (12-beat introduction on W 7615).

**PATTERN:**

PART I:   Moving forward, both do two varsouvianna steps diagonally to the left (sweeping L across R, then stepping on it diagonally forward left, and closing R to L).

Both sweep L across R, then do one varsovienne step, both moving toward center of circle with three small steps, L, R, L, as the lady crosses over in front of man, finishing with both pivoting on L, and pointing R toe to floor diagonally forward to the right.

Repeat all of Part I in reverse directions, using opposite footwork.

(Some records repeat Part I two times before music for Part II.)

PART II:   Both do the crossing over action 4 times with 4 varsovienne steps, the first to the left ending with both pointing to right, the second to the right ending with both pointing L, the third step to the left, then fourth to right.

**RHYTHMIC LEARNING CUES:**

I:   *(Diag left)*
L     L     R     L     L     R
Sweep, step, close; sweep, step, close.

"
L     L     R     L     R
Sweep, step, step, turn, point.

*(Diag right)*
R     R     L     R     R     L
Sweep, step, close; sweep, step, close.

"
R     R     L     R     L
Sweep, step, step, turn, point.

II:   *(Diag left)*
L     L     R     L     R
Sweep, step, step, turn, point.

*(Diag right)*
R     R     L     R     L
Sweep, step, step, turn, point.

*(Diag left)*
L     L     R     L     R
Sweep, step, step, turn, point.

*(Diag right)*
R     R     L     R     L
Sweep, step, step, turn, point.

**NOTE:** Part I may be done with partners facing, hands joined, arms extended sideward, man begins L, lady begins R. Some groups do a turn, turning away from each other, on the 3 steps of the varsovienne, rejoining hands for the point. Part II can be repeated as a chorus after doing the variations of Part I. In some groups 16 waltz steps are done after Part II.

# ROKOKO KOLO

JUGOSLAVIAN

Pronounced:  ROH-koh-koh

Dick Crum learned this dance in the Subotica area in Vojvodina, Jugoslavia.

Record:  Folk Dancer MH1015; KF 806-A.

**Steps:**  Slide, step-hop, stamp.

**Formation:**  No partners, closed or broken single circle or line, all facing center. Little fingers linked with neighbors, hands in W-position. Some groups use V-position for the hands.

**Timing and Rhythm:**  Two beats per slide-close (no introduction on FD MH1015).

**PATTERN:**

PART I:     Moving right (CCW), take 3 sliding steps (R, close L; R, close L; R, close L).

Step-hop R, bringing L over in front of R, and somewhat to the right of R, (almost as if doing a fourth slide, but swinging L across R, instead of closing).

PART II:     Do 10 step-hops in place, starting with L. (This should be a small movement, just a little down-up, knees loose. Men can click heels on off-beat.)

End with 3 stamps (L, R, L).

**RHYTHMIC LEARNING CUES:**

|  |  | R | R | R | R |
|---|---|---|---|---|---|
| I: | *(To right)* | Slide-ah, | slide-ah, | slide-ah, | step-hop. |

|  |  | L |  | 10 |
|---|---|---|---|---|
| II: | *(In place)* | Step-hop . . . . . . . . . . step-hop. | | |

L    R    L
Stamp, stamp, stamp.

**Styling:**  Movements are sharp and crisp. In its native setting this dance might be done by men with spurs on their boots, and the heel-clicking in Part II sets the spurs to jingling loudly. Some dancers do little backward-moving chug steps (see p. 11), instead of step-hops, in Part II.

Macedonian (Jugoslavia)

# SAPRI TAMA

ISRAELI

**Pronounced:** Sah-PREE Tah-MAH

This dance, composed by Yoav Ashriel, is based on an ancient Yemenite melody meaning "Tell me my innocent one." Described as taught by Dave Henry at East Tennessee State University Octoberfest 1969.

**Record:** Dancecraft LP 123301 Side A, Band 2.

**Steps:** Step, Yemenite.

**Formation:** No partners, free formation. For learning, everyone can face the same direction.

**Timing and Rhythm:** In Part I, mostly one beat per step, as indicated below. In Parts II and III, 2 beats per step. Four beats for the Yemenite steps. (12-beat introduction on Dancecraft LP-123301.)

**PATTERN:**

PART I:   Raise arms overhead. Step R to right while swaying to right, bend R knee while snapping fingers, step L to left while swaying to left, bend L knee while snapping fingers. (4 beats.)

Step R to right, making quarter turn to the right — CW (2 beats), close L to R bending both knees and bringing hands down in front of chest, snapping fingers (1 beat), pause (1 beat). (Total of 4 beats.)

Hands down at side. Take a Yemenite step to the right (step R to right side, bending the knee, step on ball of L beside R heel, step R across in front of L, pause). (4 beats.)

Hands still down. Take a Yemenite step to the left (step L to left, step on the ball of R by L heel, step L across in front of R, pause). (4 beats.)

PART II:   Step on R to the right, turning slightly to face right (2 beats), raise L leg across in front of R leg, bending R knee (L leg is turned out with bent knee and flexed foot), while raising hands chest-high and snapping fingers. (2 beats.) (Total of 4 beat.)

Repeat Part II with opposite footwork.

PART III:   Step on R sideward to the right, while extending the arms straight out to the sides. (2 beats.)

Step L across in front of R, bending both knees, and bringing both hands across each other in front of the chest (R hand in front of L hand). Snap fingers. (2 beats.)

Repeat stepping sideward on R, then crossing with L, while extending, and then crossing hands. (4 beats.)

Take a Yemenite step to the right. (4 beats.)

Repeat Part III, with opposite direction and footwork.

*Repeat the dance, making a quarter turn with each repetition, facing a different wall of the room with each quarter turn.*

**RHYTHMIC LEARNING CUES:**

|  |  | | Arms | Hands |
|---|---|---|---|---|
| I: | | R   R   L   L<br>Step, sway, step, sway. | Overhead | And, snap, and, snap. |
| | | R   L<br>Turn, and, close, and. | Down to chest | And, and, snap, and. |
| | (*right Yem*) | R   L   R<br>Step, step, cross, and. | Arms down | |
| | (*left Yem*) | L   R   L<br>Step, step, cross, and. | Arms down | |
| II: | | R   L<br>Step, lift. | Up to chest | And, snap. |
| | | L   R<br>Step, lift. | Up to chest | And, snap. |
| III: | (*To right*) | R   L<br>Step, cross. | Extend, cross | And, snap. |
| | | R   L<br>Step, cross. | Extend, cross | And, snap. |
| | | R   L   R<br>Step, step, cross, and. | Arms down | |

*(Repeat III, opposite directions and footwork.)*

**Styling:** Like most Israeli dances with Yemenite feeling, the dance is done with fluid grace and elegance, restrained but smooth.

# SARAJEVKA

Pronounced:  Sah-rah-YEHF-kah

A dance from the region of Sarajevo, with typical changes of tempo. Source: Dick Crum and the Hermans.

Records:  Folk Dancer MH1002; Folkraft 1496 × 45.

**Steps:**  Step, step-hop, step-touch, pas-de-bas.

**Formation:**  No partners, broken single circle, all facing somewhat right, hands joined and down in V-position.

**Timing and Rhythm:**  Two beats per step-hop (no introduction on FD MH1002).

## PATTERN:

PART I:  **Fast Music.**  Moving right (CCW), take 2 step-hops (R-hop, L-hop).

Almost in place, step sideward R, step on L behind R. End facing center.

In place, do 3 pas-de-bas or triplet steps (R-L-R, L-R-L, R-L-R).

Then turning and moving to the left (CW), take 3 walking steps (L, R, L).

Repeat Part I three more times (total 4).

PART II:  **Slow Music.**  Moving right (CCW), take 2 slow walking steps (R, L).

Almost in place, step sideward R, step on L behind R. End facing center.

In place, do 3 step-touches (R-touch L, L-touch R, R-touch L) bringing heel of touching foot about to the instep of supporting foot.

Then moving left (CW), take 3 walking steps (L, R, L).

Repeat Part II.

## RHYTHMIC LEARNING CUES:

I:  *(To CCW)*    R    L    R  L<br>
Step-hop, step-hop, step, back.

*(In place)*    R    L    R<br>
1-2-3, 1-2-3, 1-2-3

*(To CW)*    L<br>
Step, 2, 3.

*(Repeat I, total 4)*

II:  *(To CCW)*    R    L    R  L<br>
Slow, slow, quick, quick,

*(In place)*    R    L    L  R    R  L<br>
Quick-touch, step-touch, step-touch.

*(To CW)*    L<br>
Step, 2, 3.

*(Repeat II)*

**Styling:**  Some groups start dancing on the first slow music, letting the initial fast music act as an introduction. During the fast music step-hops, the joined hands can be swung lightly to about hip level. Natives of Jugoslavia would shout now and then, as they enjoy the music and dancing: Hup, hup! or Hey, Hey! or Hi, Hi! or VYEH-seh-loh!

# ŠETNJA

SERBIAN

Pronounced: SHEHT-nyah

Often the opening dance of a traditional Serbian festive occasion. Some young man, on arrival at the site of the festivities, pays the gypsy musicians to play, then starts the dance, gathering his friends one by one on his left, as he leads the dance winding in and around. Introduced by Dick Crum.

Records: Folk Dancer MH3029; Folkraft 1490.

**Steps:** Step, step-hop.

**Formation:** No partners, broken single circle. In the slower music, the left hand is held at about waist level while the right hand is hooked into the left elbow of the person to the right. In the faster music, join hands.

**Timing and Rhythm:** One beat per step, stepped off slow, slow, quick, quick, quick although the musical phrase is actually slow, slow, quick, quick, slow. (No introduction on FD MH3029.)

**PATTERN:**

PART I:    **Slow Music.** Moving and facing right (CCW), take 2 steps, R, L (slow, slow).

Continuing right, do 3 fast steps, R, L, R (quick, quick, quick). End facing center.

Moving backward away from center, take 2 steps, L, R, stepping one foot directly behind the other (slow, slow).

In place, do 3 steps, L, R, L (quick, quick quick) with the last L stepped in front of and across R.

Repeat Part I for the duration of the slower music.

PART II:    **Fast Music.** A faster version of Part I, with step-hops instead of some of the steps. When the music accelerates, join hands.

Moving and facing right, take 2 step-hops, R-hop, L-hop.

Continuing right, do 2 fast steps, R, L, and a step-hop, R-hop. End facing center.

Moving backward, take 2 step-hops, L-hop, R-hop, (stepping directly behind other foot).

More-or-less in place, take 2 steps, L, R, and a step-hop stepped across R, L-hop.

Repeat Part II until end of music.

**RHYTHMIC LEARNING CUES:**

I:    *(To CCW)*    
        R   L   R   L   R  
Slow, slow, quick, quick, quick.

   *(Bwd)*    
        L   R   L   R   L  
Slow, slow, quick, quick, cross.

*(Repeat I during slow music)*

II:    *(To CCW)*    
        R   L   R   L   R  
Slow-hop, slow-hop, quick, quick, quick-hop.

   *(Bwd)*    
        L   R   L   R   L  
Slow-hop, slow-hop, quick, quick, cross-hop.

*(Repeat II to end of music)*

# SIAMSA BEIRTE

IRISH

**Pronounced:** SHEEM-suh BERT-a

This popular Irish couple dance makes use of a number of typical Irish steps. The dance, introduced to the United States by Sean and Una O'Farrell, was learned from Mary Ann Herman.

**Records:** Folkraft 1422; Parlophone M1P 306; RCA Victor EPA 4136; or any good Irish hornpipe.

**Steps:** Step, step-hop, rocking step.

**Formation:** Partners, free information or double circle with men on the inside with backs to center, facing ladies. R hands joined at shoulder height, elbows bent and down.

**Timing and Rhythm:** One beat per step or hop (8 beat introduction on F 1422).

## PATTERN:

PART I:    **Threes and Rock.** Both moving to the man's left (man begins on L, lady on R), take 3 steps (step, behind, step), then hop (man L, lady R). Repeat to the man's right (man begins R, lady L), the 3 steps (step, behind, step), and hop (man R, lady L).

In place, both do one step-hop (man L-hop, lady R-hop), then placing the free foot behind the step-hopping foot, do another step-hop (man R-hop, lady L-hop), end with the feet on the floor, one directly in front of the other.

In place both do 3 rocking steps (man L-R-L, lady R-L-R): rise up on the balls of the feet, and without moving the feet from position, rock sideward by shifting the weight from the ball of one foot to the ball of the other foot. End with a pause.

Repeat Part I, reversing directions and footwork.

PART II:    **The Box.** Still holding R hands and moving to the man's left, both do one step, behind, step, hop (man L, R, L, hop L; lady R, L, R, hop R).

Partners then change places, still holding R hands, with a step, step, step, hop (man R, L, R, hop R; lady L, R, L, hop L) with the lady turning to her left (CCW) under the joined R hands while the man makes a half turn CW.

Repeat Part II, changing places again. The man is again on the inside of the circle.

PART III:    **Wrap around.** Now joining L hands too (R hands over, L hands under) the man rolls the joined R hands toward him, under the joined L hands, finishing with the partners close together, with the lady's arms resting on the man's arms, elbows held out horizontally, while dancing 4 step, step, step, hops, both turning CW, progress around the circle CCW.

**RHYTHMIC LEARNING CUES:**

*(Man's cues; lady opposite footwork.)*

I:     **Threes and Rock.**

*(To left)*     L     R     L     L
Step, step, step, hop.

*(To right)*     R     L     R     R
Step, step, step, hop.

*(In place)*     L     L     R     R
Step, hop, step, hop.

L     R     L
Rock, rock, rock.

*(Repeat I, but with opposite directions and footwork).*

II:     **Box.**

*(To left)*     L     R     L     L
Step, step, step, hop.

*(Changes places)*     R     L R   R
Change, 2, 3, hop.

*(To left)*     L     R     L     L
Step, step, step, hop.

*(Change places)*     R     L R   R
Change, 2, 3, hop.

III:     **Wrap Around.**

*(Turn)*     L   R   L   L   R   L   R   R
Step, step, step, hop; step, step, step, hop;

L   R   L   L   R   L   R   R
Step, step, step, hop; step, step, step, hop.

**Styling:** Light and precise. The feeling is of the "nimble feet of the Irish." The free hand hangs relaxed at the sides throughout, with very little movement.

# STEPPING OUT



What makes this a novelty dance is the interval of silence—the dancers continue the dance while the record spins in silence. Learned at the Maine Folk Dance Camp.

Record:  Blue Star 3-1528.

**Steps:**  Step, brush, step-brush.

**Formation:**  Groups (couples, trios, foursomes, etc.) side by side holding hands, all facing counterclockwise.

**Timing and Rhythm:**  Two beats per step brush, one beat per step (8-beat introduction on BS 3-1528.

**PATTERN:**

PART I:  Step on L; brush R straight forward; brush R backward across and in front of L, brush R forward.

Moving sideward to the right, take 4 steps (R, L, R, L; stepping for the L behind R).

Step on R, brush L forward, brush L backward across and in front of L, brush L forward.

Moving sideward left, take 4 steps (L, R, L, R; R behind L).

Full turn around (either right or left) with 4 step-brushes (step L, brush R, step R, brush L, step L, brush R, step R, brush L, brushing forward each time).

In place, step L, brush R forward, brush R backward across L, brush R forward. Then do 3 steps in place (R, L, R).

Repeat all of Part I.

PART II:  Moving forward, step L, pause, step R, pause, step L, pause, step R, pause, snapping fingers on each pause.

Step forward on L, and make a big circle to the side with R foot, starting backwards and bringing it around along the floor to the front (CCW). (Some groups do the circling CW.)

In place, step R, L, R.

Repeat all of Part II.

PART III:  Same as Part I. (Do only one time.)

**RHYTHMIC LEARNING CUES:**

I:    (In place)    L    R    R    R
Step, brush, brush, brush.

(To right)    R    L    R    L
Side, behind, side, behind.

(In place)    R    L    L    L
Step, brush, brush, brush.

(To left)    L    R    L    R
Side, behind, side, behind.

(Turning)    L    R    R    L    L    R    R    L
Step, brush, step, brush, step, brush, step, brush.

(In place)    L    R    R    R    R
Step, brush, brush, brush, step, 2, 3.

(Repeat I)

II:    L    R    L    R
Step, snap, step, snap, step, snap, step, snap.

L    R
Step, C - i - r - c - l - e .

R    L R
Step, 2, 3.

(Repeat II)

III:    Same as I—but one time only.

**NOTE:** When dancing the entire pattern (Part I twice, Part II twice, Part III once) the first time, there is music throughout. The second time there is no music, just rhythm. The third time there is just silence during Part I (twice) and Part II (twice). If you keep dancing a steady rhythm, when the music picks up again near the end, you'll step down with it on the left foot ready to do Part III.

# SWEDISH VARSOVIENNE



Pronounced:  Vahr-soo-vee-EHN

Many countries have a version of this varsovienne type dance. Introduced by the Swedish Folk Dance Society, this is the only form of this dance that uses the heel instead of the toe for pointing.

Records:  Folk Dancer MH1023; Folkraft 1130; Educ. Dance Record. FD-4.

Steps:  Varsovienne, mazurka, waltz.

**Formation:**  Partners, double circle, all facing counterclockwise in varsovienne position. (This is the dance the position was supposedly named after.)

**Timing and Rhythm:**  One beat per step (4-note introduction on FD MH1023 takes 8 beats).

**PATTERN:**

PART I:     Both do 4 varsovienne steps, each time changing places with 3 walking steps, lady crossing in front of partner, and ending by both placing heel diagonally forward and to the side. The first time both start L, the lady crosses to the inside of the circle, the man to the outside, and both point R heel diagonally to the right. The second time both start R, the lady crosses to the outside, man to inside, both point L heel. Continue twice more, pointing R, then L.

PART II:     Still in varsovienne position, both move forward (CCW) with 2 mazurka steps (step L forward, step R forward, then hop on R; step again with L, then R, and hop on R).

Now change places with partner with one varsovienne step (L, R, L, point R), ending man on outside, lady inside.

Repeat 2 mazurkas forward beginning with stepping R forward.

Change places again with one varsovienne step (R, L, R, point L), ending man on inside, lady outside.

PART III:     In closed or open dance position, waltz around the room 8 waltz steps.

**RHYTHMIC LEARNING CUES:**

**Floor Pattern for Part II**

I:     (*In place*)     L          R
                        Change, 2, 3, heel.

       (*In place*)     R          L
                        Change, 2, 3, heel.

                        (*Repeat I*)

II:    (*To CCW*)     L   R   R   L   R   R
                      Step, step, hop; step, step, hop.

       (*In place*)     L          R
                        Change, 2, 3, heel.

       (*To CCW*)     R   L   L   R   L   L
                      Step, step, hop; step, step, hop.

       (*In place*)     R          L
                        Change, 2, 3, heel.

III:   (*To CCW*)     Waltz, . . . . . . . 7, 8.

Man

Inside          Outside

Lady

# WALKIN' AND WHISTLIN'

AMERICAN

An enjoyable novelty dance set to a very rhythmic melody. It can be done as a couple dance or as a mixer.

Records:  Old Timer S-8150-A; Columbia 4-41696 (may be out of print but is worth hunting for).

**Steps:** Strut, step-close, two-step.

**Formation:** Partners, double circle, all facing counterclockwise, inside hands joined.

**Timing and Rhythm:** Two beats per strutting step (16-beat introduction on OT S-8150).

## PATTERN:

PART I:     Moving forward (CCW), and beginning on outside foot (man L, lady R) take 4 strutting steps.

Rock forward on outside foot, back on inside foot, forward, and back.

Repeat all of Part I.

PART II:    Face partner and join both hands. Both moving CCW, man steps sideward to his left on L, closes with R, and steps on L across R. Then he steps R to his right, closes L, and steps on R across L. Lady uses opposite footwork.

Partners turn away from each other (man to left, lady to right) with 4 two-steps, making a small circle and ending facing partner.

Repeat all of Part II.

## RHYTHMIC LEARNING CUES:

*(Man begins L, lady R throughout)*

I:       *(To CCW)*    Forward, 2, 3, 4.

                  O      I     O     I

      *(In place)*   Rock, rock, rock, rock.

*(Repeat I)*

                    CCW      CW

II:      *(Face)*    Step, close, cross.

                    CW      CCW

                    Step, close, cross.

      *(Turn)*   Two-step, 2 . , 3 . , 4 . .

*(Repeat II)*

**AS A MIXER:**  On the last part of Part II, the man circles in 4 two-steps, moving to the lady who was behind him for a new partner.

Nina Reeves of the Methodist Youth Foundation choreographed this dance.

# WEGGIS

SWISS

Pronounced:  VAY-giss

According to Michael Herman this dance was created by Robin Witschi who put together authentic figures from different cantons to be danced to the Swiss walking song, Hol-di-ri-di-a.

Records:  Folk Dancer MH1046; Folkraft 1160; World of Fun M101.

**Steps:**  Schottische, step-hop, two-step.

**Timing and Rhythm:**  Four beats per schottische step (8-beat introduction on M101).

**PATTERN:**

PART I:  **Promenade.**  Formation: Partners, double circle, facing counterclockwise, in promenade position, lady on partner's right.

With outside foot (man's L, lady's R) do a heel and toe, and one two-step (step, close, step, pause), moving forward.

With inside foot (man's R, lady's L) repeat the heel-toe and two-step forward.

Repeat all of Part I.

CHORUS:  Place both hands on own hips and take one schottische step (step, step, step, hop) sideward away from each other, the man begins L moving toward center of circle, the lady begins R moving away from the circle.

Both take a schottische step sideward back to partner (man starting R, lady L).

Partners face each other, take shoulder-waist position and turn CW with 4 step-hops (man begins L, lady on R).

Repeat all of chorus.

PART II:  **Windmill.**  Formation: Single circle, partners facing (man CCW, lady CW), both hands joined, the inside hands pointing toward center of the circle point downward, the outside hands raised high.

With inside foot, (man's L, lady's R) do a heel and toe, and a two-step toward center.

Both turn outward and point outside hands down, inside hands up, and do a heel and toe, and a two-step away from center, back to place.

Repeat all of Part II.

CHORUS:  **Repeat chorus.**

PART III:  **Step-point forward.**  Formation: Couples in promenade position, facing counterclockwise.

Both step to the left on L, point R toe across L, then step R to the right, and point L toe across R.

Do 2 two-steps forward, beginning L.

Repeat all of Part III.

CHORUS:  **Repeat chorus.**

PART IV:    **Step-point face.** Formation: Partners face each other in a double circle, with right hands joined and held high. Man's back to center of circle.

Both step to left on L, point R toe across L, then step R to the right, and point L toe across R. Both move CW into partner's position with two-steps, beginning L.

Repeat the step-points and two-steps and return to original places.

CHORUS:    **Repeat chorus.**

PART V:    **Turn.** Formation: Partners face each other, in a double circle, man's right hand and lady's left hand joined and extended to the side at shoulder level. Man's back to center of circle.

Both take 3 walking steps forward (CCW), (man begins L, lady R), turning once around (man to left, lady to right). End facing partner with other hands joined and bow and curtsy. (For a little momentum swing the hands downward and forward at the beginning of the turns.)

Take 3 walking steps (CW) turning back to place (man to right, lady to left), and swinging hands. Bow and curtsy.

Repeat all of Part V.

CHORUS:    **Repeat chorus.**


**RHYTHMIC LEARNING CUES:**

I:    **Promenade.**        *(Man begin L, lady R)*

   *(To CCW)*    Heel, and, toe, and, step, close, step.

   *"*    Heel, and, toe, and, step, close, step.


   *(Repeat I)*

**Chorus.**        *(Man begin L, lady R)*


   *(Apart)*    Step, step, step, hop.

   *(Together)*    Step, step, step, hop.

   *(Turn)*    Step-hop, step-hop, step-hop, step-hop.


   *(Repeat Chorus)*


II:    **Windmill.**        *(Man begin L, lady R)*

   *(To center)*    Heel, and, toe, and, step, close, step.

   *(To wall)*    Heel, and, toe, and, step, close, step.


   *(Repeat II)*


**Chorus.**

III:     **Step-Point Fwd.**     *(Both begin L)*

*(To CCW)*     L      R    R     L
           Step, and, point, step, and, point.

Step, close, step; step, close, step.

*(Repeat III)*

**Chorus.**

IV:     **Step-point face.**     *(Both begin L)*

*(In place)*     L     R   L     R
          Step, and, point, step, and, point.

*(Turn CW)*     Step, close, step; step, close, step.

*(Repeat IV)*

**Chorus.**

V:     **Turns.**     *(Man begins L, lady R)*

*(To CCW)*     Turn, step, step, bow.

*(To CW)*     Turn, step, step, bow.

*(Repeat V)*

**Chorus.**

Here is one version of the song for those who like to sing as they dance:

From Lucerne to Weggis on
Hol-di-ri-di-a, hol-di-ri-di-a
Shoes nor stockings need we don
Hol-di-ri-di-a, hol-di-a

Chorus:

Hol-di-ri-di-a
Hol-di-ri-di-a, hol-di-ri-a
Hol-di-ri-di-a
Hol-di-ri-di-a, hol-di-a

On the lake we all shall go,
Hol-di-ri-di-a, hol-di-ri-a
See the pretty fish below
Hol-di-ri-di-a, hol-di-a

Repeat Chorus

Weggis starts the highest hill,
Hol-di-ri-di-a, hol-di-ri-a
Boys and girls, shout "hop-sa-saa"
Hol-di-ri-di-a, hol-di-a

Repeat Chorus

# *Appendix*

Macedonian (Jugoslavia)

# GLOSSARY

**Bounce** — Springing up just enough to get the heels off the floor.

**Brush** — Touch the floor lightly with the ball while kicking the free foot.

**Buzz** — Lead with one foot while pushing with the other foot.

**"Charleston"** — Step L fwd, point R fwd, step R back, point L bwd.

**Chug** — Fall fwd on the lead foot while pushing off with the trailing foot. Then close with trailing foot.

**Another Chug** — With weight on one or both feet, move that foot (or feet) a short distance across the floor.

**Close** — Bring the free foot up to the supporting foot and shift weight to it.

**Corner** — The man's corner is the lady to his left. The lady's corner is the man on her right.

**Galop** — Leap with one foot and quickly close other foot to it.

**Glide** — The ball of the advancing foot makes a long sliding contact with the floor as in skating.

**Grapevine** — (Left) Step R across L, step L to the left, step R behind L, step L to the left. Grapevine (Right) with opposite footwork.

**Heel and Toe** — Touch one heel to the floor, then the toe of the same foot.

**Hop** — Lightly jump off the floor from one foot and land on same foot.

**Hop-Point** — Hop and at same time point the other foot.

**Hop-swing** — Hop on supporting foot and swing free foot.

**In place** — The spot or place you were in when the movement began.

**Inside foot or hand** — The one closest to your partner.

**Jump** — Spring off the floor and land with the feet together.

**Kick** — With weight on one foot, thrust the other foot in the specified direction.

**Leap** — Spring from one foot to the other.

**Mazurka** — Step L, step R, hop R. Continue with same lead foot.

**Old Time Dance** — A dance made up of a mixture of folk and ballroom steps and movements.

**Outside foot or hand** — The one farthest from your partner.

**Pas-de-bas** — Leap L, step R, step L. Continue with opposite footwork.

**Pivot** — Weight on one foot, turn quickly and smoothly to face the opposite direction.

**Point** — Touch the free toe to the floor in any direction.

**Polka** — Hop L, step R, close L, step R. Continue with opposite footwork.

**Run** — Rhythmical transfer of weight from one foot to the other but for just a brief moment both feet are off the floor.

**Schottische** — Step L, close R, step L, hop L; or run L, run R, run L, hop L. Continue with opposite footwork.

**Slide** — Step to the side and quickly bring up the other foot and shift weight to it.

**Stamp** — Strike the floor vigorously with the foot.

**Step** — Place one foot on the floor and shift weight to it.

**Step-brush** — Step on one foot and lightly swing the other foot forward making contact with the floor.

**Step-close** — Step to the side, bring other foot up to it and transfer weight.

**Step-draw** — Step to one side, then lightly drag the other foot to it and transfer weight.

**Step-hop** — Step on one foot, then hop on it.

**Step-point** — Step on one foot and point the free foot.

**Step-swing** — Step on one foot, swing the other foot lightly in the direction specified for the dance.

**Strut** — To walk with a swagger, exaggerate the bend in the knee when walking.

**Swivel** — Keep both feet together, move both toes in one direction, and then the heels in the same direction. Sometimes called *Suzie-Q.*

**Three** — Quickly step L-R-L or R-L-R, almost in place.

**Two-step** — Step L, close R, step L, pause. Continue by alternating lead foot.

**Varsouvianna** — Sweep L in front of R, step L diagonally to side, close R to L.

**Varsovienne** — Step L, step R, step L, point R, pause. Continue with opposite footwork.

**Walk** — Rhythmical transfer of weight from one foot to the other. One foot always remains in contact with the floor.

**Waltz** — Step L, step R, close L. Continue by alternating lead foot.

**Waltz-balance** — Step L, step-rise R, step L. Continue with opposite footwork.

# FOLK DANCE RECORD SUPPLIERS

The record suppliers listed below are reported as keeping a large stock of folk dance records and can supply them without delay.

1. Festival Records
   161 Turk Street
   San Francisco, California 94102

2. Folk Dance House
   P. O. Box 201
   Flushing, New York 11352

3. Folkraft Records
   1159 Broad Street
   Newark, New Jersey 07114

4. Folk Music International (Worldtone)
   56-40 187th Street
   Flushing, New York 11365

5. The Record Center
   2581 Piedmont Road, N. E.
   Atlanta, Georgia 30324

6. The Record Center
   1614 N. Pulaski Street
   Chicago, Illinois 60639

7. Canadian F.D.S. Audio Visual
   185 Spadina Avenue
   Toronto 2B, Ontario, Canada

8. BOZ-OK Records (for Turkish records only)
   P. O. Box 9051
   Berkeley, California 74709

# FOLK DANCE BIBLIOGRAPHY

The following books will be of help if you desire additional information. Some give comprehensive descriptions of basic steps, formation, teaching methods, and the history of folk dance.


Duggan, Anne, Jeanette Schlottmann, and Abbie Rutledge, *The Folk Dance Library*, New York: Ronald Press, 1948. 4 volumes.

Fox, Grace I., *Folk Dancing in High School and College*, New York: A. S. Barnes and Co., 1944.

Gilbert, Cecile, *International Folk Dance at A Glance*, Minneapolis: Burgess Publishing Co., 1974.

Hall, Tillman J., *Dance*, Belmont, California: Wadsworth Publishing Co., Inc., 1963.

Hall, Tillman J., *Folk Dance*, Pacific Palisades, California: Goodyear Publishing Co., 1969.

Harris, Jane, Annie Pittman, and Marilyn S. Waller, *Dance A While*, Minneapolis: Burgess Publishing Co., 1968.

Herman, Michael, *Folk Dance Syllabus, No. 1*, New York: Folk Dance House, 1953.

Herman, Michael, *Folk Dances for All*, New York: Barnes and Noble, 1948.

Hipps, Harold and Wallace Chappell, *A World of Fun*, Nashville, Tennessee: Methodist Publishing House, 1959.

Jensen, Mary Bee and Jensen, Clayne R., *Folk Dancing*, Provo, Utah: Brigham Young University Press, 1973.

Jensen, Mary Bee and Jensen, Clayne R., *Beginning Folk Dancing*, Provo, Utah: Brigham Young University Press, (Rev. Ed.) 1973.

Joukowsky, Anatol, *The Teaching of Ethnic Dance*, New York: J. Lowell Pratt and Co., 1965.

Kraus, Richard, *Folk Dancing*, New York: The Macmillan Co., 1962.

Lidster, Miriam D., and Dorothy H. Tamburini, *Folk Dance Progressions*, Belmont, California: Wadsworth Publishing Co., Inc., 1965.

Spiesman, M. C., *Folk Dancing*, Philadelphia: W. B. Saunders Co., 1970.

Wakefield, Eleanor Ely, *Folk Dancing in America*, New York: J. Lowell Pratt and Co., 1966.


# PERIODICALS

These magazines, the leaders in the folk dance area, provide an opportunity to keep up with current developments.

1. *Let's Dance.* Published by the California Folk Dance Federation, 1095 Market Street, Room 213, San Francisco, California 94103. Ten issues per year.
2. *Northern Junket.* Published by Ralph Page, 117 Washington Street, Keene, New Hampshire 03431. Monthly.
3. *Viltis.* Published by Vyts Beliajus, P.O. Box 1226, Denver, Colorado 80201. Six issues per year.

# NUMBER OF DANCERS AND LEVEL OF DIFFICULTY

| *Non-Partner* | *Couple* | *3 or More* |
|---|---|---|
| Ali Paşa (M) * | American Schottische (M) * | Appalachian Big Circle (E) |
| Alley Cat (E) | Apat-Apat (E) | Black Nag (M) |
| Alunelul (M) | Black Hawk Waltz (M) | Crested Hen (E) |
| Amos Moses (E) | Bossa Nova (M) | D'Hammerschmiedsg'selln (M) |
| Bele Kawe (E) | Boston Two-Step (E) | Hot Pretzels (E) |
| Cherkassiya (M) | Cotton-Eyed Joe (M) | Limbo Rock (M) |
| Ciuleandra (M) | Doudlebska Polka (E) | Raksi Jaak (E) |
| Harmonica (M) | Fado Blanquito (M) | Salty Dog Rag (E) |
| Hasapikos (E) | Gay Gordons (E) | Stepping Out (M) |
| Hashual (E) | Good Old Days (E) | Texas Schottische (E) |
| Hora (E) | Hip Hip Polka (E) | Troika (E) |
| Hora Medura (E) | Java (E) | Twelfth Street Rag (E) |
| Ivanica (E) | Kalvelis (M) | |
| Jugo (E) | Korobushka (M) | |
| Kendime (E) | Lili Marlene (E) | |
| Kuma Echa (M) | Limbo Rock (M) | |
| Lech Lech Lamidbar (M) | Mexican Mixer (E) | |
| Limbo Rock (M) | Oslo Waltz (M) | |
| Mayim (M) | Ostende (E) | |
| Nebesko Kolo (M) | Put Your Little Foot (M) | |
| Neda Grivne (E) | St. Bernard Waltz (E) | |
| Never on Sunday (M) | Salty Dog Rag (E) | |
| Orijent (M) | Siamsa Beirte (M) | |
| Pata Pata (M) | Stepping Out (M) | * (E) Easy to learn |
| Pleskavac (E) | Swedish Varsovienne (M) | * (M) Moderately easy to learn |
| Polster Tanc (E) | Tant' Hessie (E) | |
| Poskok (E) | Tennessee Wig Walk (E) | |
| Rokoko Kolo (M) | Teton Mountain Stomp (E) | |
| Salty Dog Rag (E) | Texas Schottische (E) | |
| Sapri Tama (M) | Twelfth Street Rag (E) | |
| Sarajevka (M) | V'David (E) | |
| Savila Se Bela Loza (E) | Walkin' and Whistlin' (M) | |
| Şeljančica (E) | Weggis (M) | |
| Setnja (M) | Wooden Shoes (E) | |
| Shiboleth Basadeh (E) | Zigeunerpolka (E) | |
| Snoopy (E) | | |
| Soultana (E) | | |
| Stepping Out (M) | | |
| Syrtos (E) | | |
| Twelfth Street Rag (E) | | |
| Tzadik Katamar (E) | | |
| Zaječarka (E) | | |

# MIXER AND NOVELTY DANCES

## MIXER

*Name and Page*

Apat Apat, 21
Boston Two-Step, 28
Cotton-Eyed Joe, 83
Doudlebska Polka, 30
Gay Gordons, 31
Good Old Days, 32
Hip Hip Polka, 36
Java, 40
Kalvelis, 91
Lili Marlene, 43
Mexican Mixer, 44
Oslo Waltz, 105
Ostende, 46

*Name and Page*

Polster Tanc, 48
Salty Dog Rag, 52
St. Bernard Waltz, 51
Tant' Hessie, 60
Tennessee Wig Walk, 61
Teton Mountain Stomp, 62
Texas Schottische, 63
Troika, 65
V'David, 68
Walkin' and Whistlin', 118
Wooden Shoes, 69
Zigeunerpolka, 72

## AMERICAN NOVELTY

*Name and Page*

Alley Cat, 19
Amos Moses, 20
Bossa Nova, 81
Good Old Days, 32
Java, 40
Limbo Rock, 97
Salty Dog Rag, 52
Snoopy, 57
Stepping Out, 115
Tennessee Wig Walk, 61
Twelfth Street Rag, 66
Walkin' and Whistlin, 118

# SELECTED DANCES CLASSIFIED ACCORDING TO PREDOMINANT BASIC STEP AND LEVEL OF DIFFICULTY

### Walk

Apat-Apat (E)*
Appalachian Big Circle (E)
Lili Marlene (E)
Mexican Mixer (E)
Neda Grivne (E)
Pleskavac (E)
Seljančica (E)
Syrtos (E)
Tant' Hessie (E)
Teton Mountain Stomp (E)
Texas Schottische (E)
V'David (E)

### Step-Hop

Crested Hen (E)
D'Hammerschmiedsg'selln (M)
Harmonica (M)
Rokoko Kolo (M)
Salty Dog Rag (E)
Şarajevka (M)
Šetnja (M)
Shibolet Basadeh (E)
Siamsa Beirte (M)

### Grapevine

Cherkassiya (M)
Ciuleandra (M)
Harmonica (M)
Hashual (E)
Hora Medura (E)
Kuma Echa (M)
Lech Lech Lamidbar (M)
Mayim (M)
Tzadik Katamar (E)

### Two-Step

Bossa Nova (M)*
Boston Two-Step (E)
Cotton-Eyed Joe (M)
Gay Gordons (E)
Lili Marlene (E)
Limbo Rock (M)
Nebesko Kolo (M)
Texas Schottische (E)
Walkin' and Whistlin' (M)
Weggis (M)

### Polka

Doudlebska Polka (E)
Hip-Hip Polka (E)
Kalvelis (M)
Polster Tanc (E)
Raksi Jaak (M)
Wooden Shoes (E)
Zigeunerpolka (E)

### Schottische

American Schottische (M)
Fado Blanquito (M)
Korobushka (M)
Kuma Echa (M)
Ostende (E)
Poskok (E)
Salty Dog Rag (E)
Savila Se Bela Loza (E)
Tennessee Wig Walk (E)
Weggis (M)

### Waltz

Black Hawk Waltz (M)
D'Hammerschmiedsg'selln (M)
Oslo Waltz (M)
Polster Tanc (E)
St. Bernard Waltz (E)
Swedish Varsovienne (M)

* (E) Easy to learn
* (M) Moderately easy to learn

# DANCE NATIONALITY

*Name and Page*

American, 19, 20, 22, 32, 40, 43, 46, 52,
   57, 61, 62, 63, 66, 77, 78, 81, 83, 97,
   106, 107, 115, 118
Balkan, 41
Creole-African, 26
Czechoslovakian, 30
Danish, 29
English, 28, 51, 79
Estonian, 50
German, 72, 86
Greek, 33, 58, 59
Greek-American, 101
Irish, 113
Israeli, 34, 37, 38, 56, 67, 68, 82, 89, 94,
   95, 99, 109
Jugoslavian, 39, 108
Lithuanian, 36, 69, 91

*Name and Page*

Mexican, 44
Philippine, 21
Portuguese-Brazilian, 87
Romanian, 76, 84
Romanian-American, 47
Russian, 65
Russian-American, 93
Scotch-English, 105
Scottish, 31
Serbian, 45, 49, 54, 55, 71, 100, 103, 111, 112
Slovenian, 48
South African, 60
Swedish, 117
Swiss-American, 119
Turkish, 42, 74

# CLASSIFIED INDEX OF DANCES

| Name of Dance | Page | Nationality | Number of dancers | Basic Steps | Level of difficulty |
|---|---|---|---|---|---|
| Ali Paşa | 74 | Turkish | no-partner | step, point, brush | moderate |
| Alley Cat | 19 | American | no-partner | step, touch, jump | easy |
| Alunelul | 76 | Romanian | no-partner | step, stamp | moderate |
| American Schottische | 77 | American | couple | schottische, step-hop | moderate |
| Amos Moses | 20 | American | no-partner | touch, step | easy |
| Apat-Apat | 21 | Philippine | couple | walk | easy |
| Appalachian Big Circle | 22 | American | couple | walk | easy |
| Bele Kawe | 26 | Creole-African | no-partner | step, touch | easy |
| Black Hawk Waltz | 78 | American | couple | waltz, step, point | moderate |
| Black Nag | 79 | English | 3 couples | run, slide, skip | moderate |
| Bossa Nova | 81 | American | couple | two-step, Charleston, step, point | moderate |
| Boston Two-Step | 28 | English | couple | walk, slide, two-step, pas-de-bas | easy |
| Cherkassiya | 82 | Israeli | no-partner | grapevine | moderate |
| Cotton-Eyed Joe | 83 | American | couple | two-step, chug, heel & toe | moderate |
| Crested Hen | 29 | Danish | trio | step-hop | easy |
| Ciuleandra | 84 | Romanian | no-partner | step, grapevine, stamp | moderate |
| D'Hammerschmiedsg'selln | 86 | German | 2 couples | step-hop, waltz, step | moderate |
| Doudlebska Polka | 30 | Czechoslovakian | couple | polka, walk | easy |
| Fado Blanquito | 87 | Portuguese-Brazilian | couple | schottische, run, jump | moderate |
| Gay Gordons | 31 | Scottish | couple | walk, two-step, pas-de-bas | easy |
| Good Old Days | 32 | American | couple | walk, Charleston | easy |
| Harmonica | 89 | Israeli | no-partner | grapevine, step-hop, leap, run | moderate |
| Hasapikos | 33 | Greek | no-partner | step, step-swing | easy |
| Hashual | 34 | Israeli | no-partner | step, grapevine, two-step, brush | easy |
| Hip Hip Polka | 36 | Lithuanian | couple | polka, two-step | easy |
| Hora | 37 | Israeli | no-partner | step-swing, step | easy |
| Hora Medura | 38 | Israeli | no-partner | grapevine, slide | easy |
| Ivanica | 39 | Jugoslavian | no-partner | step | easy |
| Java | 40 | American | couple | strut, jump, step | easy |
| Jugo | 41 | Balkan | no-partner | walk, leap, point | easy |
| Kalvelis | 91 | Lithuanian | couple | polka, stamp, skip | moderate |
| Kendime | 42 | Turkish | no-partner | step, touch | easy |
| Korobushka | 93 | Russian-American | couple | schottische, step-hop, walk | moderate |
| Kuma Echa | 94 | Israeli | no-partner | schottische, grapevine, run | moderate |
| Lech Lech Lamidbar | 95 | Israeli | no-partner | step, leap, jump, grapevine, hop | moderate |
| Lili Marlene | 43 | American | couple | walk, slide, two-step | easy |
| Limbo Rock | 97 | American | any number | step, two-step | moderate |
| Mayim | 99 | Israeli | no-partner | grapevine, walk, hop, point | moderate |
| Mexican Mixer | 44 | Mexican | couple | walk, step-swing, balance | easy |

| Name of Dance | Page | Nationality | Number of dancers | Basic Steps | Level of difficulty |
|---|---|---|---|---|---|
| Nebesko Kolo | 100 | Serbian | no-partner | two-step, step, threes | moderate |
| Neda Grivne | 45 | Serbian | no-partner | walk, balance | easy |
| Never on Sunday | 101 | Greek-American | no-partner | step, pivot, point & brush | moderate |
| Orijent | 103 | Serbian | no-partner | step, point | moderate |
| Oslo Waltz | 105 | Scottish-English | couple | waltz, waltz-balance, step-draw | moderate |
| Ostende | 46 | American | couple | schottische, glide, step-hop | easy |
| Pata Pata | 106 | American | no-partner | touch, step, kick | moderate |
| Pleskavac | 47 | Romanian-American | no-partner | step, stamp | easy |
| Polster Tanc | 48 | Slovenian | no-partner | polka, waltz | easy |
| Poskok | 49 | Serbian | no-partner | step, hop, schottische | easy |
| Put Your Little Foot | 107 | American | couple | varsouvianna-mazurka, varsovienne | moderate |
| Raksi Jaak | 50 | Estonian | trio | polka, walk | easy |
| Rokoko Kolo | 108 | Jugoslavian | no-partner | slide, step-hop, stamp | moderate |
| St. Bernard Waltz | 51 | English | couple | waltz, step-draw, walk | easy |
| Salty Dog Rag | 52 | American | any number | schottische, step-hop, step-brush | easy |
| Sapri Tama | 109 | Israeli | no-partner | step | moderate |
| Sarajevka | 111 | Serbian | no-partner | step, step-hop, pas-de-bas | moderate |
| Savila Se Bela Loza | 54 | Serbian | no-partner | schottische, run | easy |
| Šeljančica | 55 | Serbian | no-partner | step, walk | easy |
| Setnja | 112 | Serbian | no-partner | step, step-hop | moderate |
| Shibolet Basadeh | 56 | Israeli | no-partner | slide, step-hop | easy |
| Siamsa Beirte | 113 | Irish | couple | step, step-hop | moderate |
| Snoopy | 57 | American | no-partner | step, touch, kick | easy |
| Soultana | 58 | Greek | no-partner | step, touch, run, jump, hop | easy |
| Stepping Out | 115 | American | any number | step, brush, step-brush | moderate |
| Swedish Varsovienne | 117 | Swedish | couple | varsovienne, mazurka, waltz | moderate |
| Syrtos | 59 | Greek | no-partner | step | easy |
| Tant' Hessie | 60 | South African | couple | walk, buzz-step | easy |
| Tennessee Wig Walk | 61 | American | couple | schottische, walk, heel-toe | easy |
| Teton Mountain Stomp | 62 | American | couple | step, stamp, walk | easy |
| Texas Schottische | 63 | American | trio/couple | two-step, walk, heel-toe | easy |
| Troika | 65 | Russian | trio | run, stamp | easy |
| Twelfth Street Rag | 66 | American | any number | strut, Charleston, point, step | easy |
| Tzadik Katamar | 67 | Israeli | no-partner | step, grapevine | easy |
| V'David | 68 | Israeli | couple | walk, buzz-step | easy |
| Walkin' and Whistlin' | 118 | American | couple | strut, two-step, step-close | moderate |
| Weggis | 119 | Swiss-American | couple | schottische, step-hop, two-step | moderate |
| Wooden Shoes | 69 | Lithuanian | couple | walk, stamp, polka | easy |
| Zaječarka | 71 | Serbian | no-partner | walk, threes, step-touch | easy |
| Zigeunerpolka | 72 | German | couple | polka, walk | easy |